AMAZING STORIES®

GREAT CANADIAN IMPOSTERS

For Bob, who understands that "many people will not listen to simple truths except when uttered by exotic personalities."

Comments on other *Amazing Stories* from readers & reviewers

"*You might call them the non-fiction response to Harlequin romances: easy to consume and potentially addictive.*"
Robert Martin, *The Chronicle Herald*

"*Tightly written volumes filled with lots of wit and humour about famous and infamous Canadians.*"
Eric Shackleton, *The Globe and Mail*

"*This is popular history as it should be ... For this price, buy two and give one to a friend.*"
Terry Cook, a reader from Ottawa, on **Rebel Women**

"*Stories are rich in description, and bristle with a clever, stylish realness.*"
Mark Weber, *Central Alberta Advisor*, on **Ghost Town Stories II**

"*The resulting book is one readers will want to share with all the women in their lives.*"
Lynn Martel, *Rocky Mountain Outlook*, on **Women Explorers**

"[The books are] *long on plot and character and short on the sort of technical analysis that can be dreary for all but the most committed academic.*"
Robert Martin, *The Chronicle Herald*

"*A compelling read. Bertin ... has selected only the most intriguing tales, which she narrates with a wealth of detail.*"
Joyce Glasner, *New Brunswick Reader*, on **Strange Events**

"*The heightened sense of drama and intrigue, combined with a good dose of human interest, is what sets* Amazing Stories *apart.*"
Pamela Klaffke, *Calgary Herald*

AMAZING STORIES®

GREAT CANADIAN IMPOSTERS

Millionaires, doctors, aboriginal heroes,
and stars of stage and screen —
pretenders all

by Cheryl MacDonald

James Lorimer & Company Ltd., Publishers
Toronto

James Lorimer & Company Ltd., Publishers acknowledge the support of the Ontario Arts Council. We acknowledge the support of the Government of Canada through the Book Publishing Industry Development Program (BPIDP) for our publishing activities. We acknowledge the support of the Canada Council for the Arts for our publishing program. We acknowledge the support of the Government of Ontario through the Ontario Media Development Corporation's Ontario Book Initiative.

Canada Council
for the Arts

ONTARIO ARTS COUNCIL
CONSEIL DES ARTS DE L'ONTARIO

Library and Archives Canada Cataloguing in Publication

MacDonald, Cheryl, 1952-
Great Canadian imposters: millionaires, doctors, aboriginal heroes and stars of stage and screen — pretenders all / Cheryl MacDonald.

(Amazing stories)
ISBN 978-1-55277-411-3

1. Impostors and imposture—Canada—Biography.
2. Impostors and imposture—Canada—History.
I. Title. II. Series: Amazing stories (Toronto, Ont.)

CT9980.M33 2009   364.16'3   C2009-900451-8

James Lorimer & Company Ltd., Publishers
317 Adelaide Street West, Suite 1002
Toronto, Ontario
M5V 1P9
www.lorimer.ca

Printed and bound in Canada

Mixed Sources
Cert no. SW-COC-001271
© 1996 FSC

FSC

Contents

Prologue

As the destroyer pitched up and down in heavy seas, the young surgeon examined his patient. One of nearly 20 South Korean combatants wounded in recent fighting, the man was seriously injured. The surgeon studied the frail, malnourished body and the bullet wound in his chest.

Nothing in his experience had prepared the 29-year-old for what he was about to attempt. In spite of his position as a naval surgeon-lieutenant, his track record in the operating theatre was non-existent. He had, of course, kept this fact from his superiors and crew members. Indeed, the naval men now crowded around him would have been horrified had they any inkling of the truth. Since joining the navy, this "surgeon" had gained most of his knowledge of medical practice from the textbooks he studied endlessly.

In the past six months, Fred Demara had avoided surgery as much as possible, usually by turning his patients over to another doctor. Today, there was no option. Without surgery, the Korean would die. To save the soldier — and his own reputation — he had to proceed, especially with so many of his crew mates watching.

He picked up the scalpel and nodded to the two men who were assisting him. Calmly, as though he had cut into living human flesh hundreds of times, he brought the blade to the man's chest and made the incision.

Chapter 1

The Fur-Trader:
Isabel Gunn

I n late December 1807, fur traders in the Canadian northwest were startled to discover that one of their colleagues
was a woman. Employees of the Hudson's Bay Company
had never heard of such a thing — but then, they had never
reckoned with the devotion and determination of Isabel
Gunn.

Her curious adventure began in Stromness, Scotland, in
the spring of 1806. It was much like every other spring in the
small port. As usual, the Orkney Islands town welcomed the
outbound fleet of the Hudson's Bay Company. And, as usual,
a number of Orcadian men signed on with the company for
terms of three or five years in the Canadian northwest. The
hardy inhabitants of these islands were not afraid of facing
the harsh Canadian climate, as their own land was almost as
inhospitable.

The Orkneys are a group of 65 islands off the northeast
tip of Scotland. Located nearly as far north as Whitehorse, the
capital of the Yukon, they are rocky and windswept, with soil
so poor that few farms flourish and trees are rare. Historically,

many Orcadians were forced to leave to seek work: the women as servants in more southerly British communities, the men as fishermen or fur traders.

Around 1702, the Hudson's Bay Company began hiring Orcadians. By the early 1800s, they accounted for three-quarters of the "servants," or regular labourers, employed by the Hudson's Bay Company. For many years, the company had experienced difficulties in finding suitable employees. Most men in London, where the company's headquarters were located, were generally unsuited for the harsh climate of the Canadian north. In addition, the company had to compete with the Royal Navy, which forcibly drafted the strongest and healthiest men into the service of the Crown.

The solution to the employment problem presented itself on the outward voyage to Canada. Typically, Company ships left London as early in the year as weather conditions allowed, sailing down the Thames to Gravesend, then turning northward and following the eastern coastline of England and Scotland, before looping into the Orkneys. Stromness was the last place where company ships could load fresh water — and the final spot for hiring men to work in Canada.

The arrival of the Hudson's Bay ships was cause for celebration. Stromness took on a festive atmosphere when the ships were in port, with dinners, receptions, and balls most nights. There was always a certain optimism, for a man who completed his term in Canada had a good chance of coming home with enough money to live comfortably for many years. Yet there was also an air of sadness at the festivities, as parents, wives, or sweethearts said farewell to the men, knowing that it would be at least three years before they met again.

One of those sweethearts was not willing to wait that long to see her man again. Isabel Gunn, a feisty young woman, made up her mind to follow her lover to Canada. Disguising herself as a boy, she used the name John Fubbister and signed on for a three-year term with the Hudson's Bay Company at an annual salary of £8.

Isabel's disguise certainly fooled company officials, but it is not likely that she fooled her co-workers. Secrets are difficult to keep in small, tightly knit communities like the Orkneys, and even more difficult in the close quarters of a ship, where passengers spent nearly every moment together. But Orcadians could be extremely tight-lipped, as explorer and Hudson's Bay Company fur trader Samuel Hearne revealed. Although he had considerable respect for them, "the quietest servants and the best adapted for this country that can be procured," Hearne knew their faults from personal experience.

"They are the slyest set of men under the sun and their universal propensity to smuggling, and clandestine dealings of every kind, added to their clannish attachment to each other, puts it out of the power of any one Englishman to detect them."

If the lovers had been posted to the same area, the

Orcadians' clannishness might have helped keep them together. However, the Hudson's Bay Company sent the young man to Eastmain, Quebec, while Isabel went to Fort Albany, on the Ontario side of James Bay.

Now that her plans had been thwarted, Isabel had to make a choice. She could reveal her identity and be sent home in disgrace on the next ship. Or she could hide her disappointment, continue her masquerade, and fulfill the conditions of her three-year contract. Possibly motivated as much by profit as by the chance of a reunion with her lover, Isabel maintained her disguise.

Like other servants of the Hudson's Bay Company, Isabel was expected to carry out a range of tasks, including moving trade goods from fur-trading posts to inland locations. It was hard, burdensome work. They packed heavy loads into boats and negotiated rivers and streams that were often either swollen from floods or so low that it was necessary to lift the canoes over rocks. But it was all part of a day's work.

Sir John Franklin, the famous explorer who died in the Arctic in 1847, was amazed by the Orcadians' ability to move in and out of freezing cold water, work all day in near-zero temperatures while wearing wet clothing, and carry heavy burdens. Isabel was expected to do all these things. She met those expectations, and "worked at anything & well like the rest of the men," according to Hudson's Bay Company records.

But life was not a constant grind. Although Company servants had to work very hard, they were able to relax when there were no pressing jobs to be done. They would hunt or fish, skate or snowshoe, and — of course — gamble. Cards and dice were always popular pastimes. There were also various social occasions throughout the year, including dances to which Native women were frequently invited. Whether Isabel enjoyed the manly pursuits or attended the dances is not known. However, it is likely she welcomed the respite from the backbreaking work.

Isabel's secret might have gone undiscovered until her contract was up, but other circumstances intervened. By the late spring of 1807, she was pregnant by another fur trader, John Scarth. Amazingly, she managed to conceal her pregnancy right up to the end.

At the time, Isabel was stationed in Pembina (now in North Dakota). It was the Christmas season, and on December 29 the Hudson's Bay crew paid a social visit to their counterparts at a nearby North West Company outpost. But, as they were preparing to leave, "John Fubbister" complained of feeling poorly and asked to stay behind.

It was an unusual request, but Alexander Henry, the man in charge of the post, graciously extended the hospitality of the establishment. He told Fubbister to go inside and get warm. Then Henry returned to his own quarters. A short time later, one of the North West Company employees knocked on the door of Henry's room and informed him that Fubbister wanted to speak to him. Henry recorded what happened next:

> *I stepped down to him, and was much surprised to find him extended on the hearth, uttering dreadful lamentations; he stretched out his hands toward me, and in piteous tones begged to me to be kind to a poor, helpless, abandoned wretch, who was not of the sex I had supposed, but an unfortunate Orkney girl, pregnant, and actually in childbirth. In saying this she opened her jacket, and displayed a pair of beautiful, round white breasts; she further informed me of the circumstances that had brought her into this state.*

Henry's account states that she gave birth to a "fine boy" within an hour. A short time later, Henry put her and the baby in his own horse-drawn sleigh and had them driven to the Hudson's Bay post.

Within a short time, Isabel was ready to get back to work, and probably continued her regular duties while she remained at Pembina. In the spring of 1808, she returned to Fort Albany. However, now that her sex was known, she was not allowed to resume her regular duties. Native women were actively engaged in the fur trade helping prepare skins, making and maintaining clothing and equipment, sometimes negotiating prices, and cementing relations through their marriages to white men. But Hudson's Bay Company rules forbade white women from working at outposts.

With London and the top company officials far away, John Hodgson, the chief factor at Fort Albany, made the best of the situation. He was already familiar with Isabel's abilities, but there was no question of her continuing to work alongside the men. Instead, she was assigned duties as a washerwoman, a task she hated. She may also have worked as nursemaid, caring for the children of the traders and their Native wives.

In the fall of 1809, when Isabel's son was nearly two, he was baptized by the schoolmaster. Isabel and the boy should actually have been sent home when the supply ship left earlier that year, but she did not want to return to the Orkney Islands. Hodgson was sympathetic, but he was bound by company regulations. The following year, he had no choice but to order Isabel aboard the ship bound for Stromness.

What happened to her when she arrived in Scotland is unclear. As a single woman with a child born out of wedlock, she was probably ostracized to some extent. What may have made her more of a social outcast was that she had disguised herself and lived as a man for more than a year. According to traditional accounts, Isabel became a vagrant and a prostitute and died in poverty.

If the stories are true, it was a sad ending for a woman whose determination and devotion had taken her halfway around the world, to the harsh wilderness of the Canadian northwest.

Chapter 2
The Medical Man: James Barry

James Barry was a flamboyant character, well-known in the British military's tight network of friendships and rivalries for his steely determination. He became an army doctor in 1816, and served in remote and exotic locations around the world for the next 40 years.

In his first important posting, in Cape Town, South Africa, he made a name for himself — and ruffled a few feathers — by introducing sweeping reforms in army medical care. He also looked after lepers, fought for the regulation of medical licenses and drugs, and campaigned for public health.

A short, delicate-looking man with small hands and a high-pitched voice, Barry's zeal and bombastic attitude contrasted sharply with his appearance. His personality earned him a lot of enemies, but he also acquired powerful friends, including Governor-General Lord Charles Somerset. The young doctor had saved Somerset's life, and the men became very close. In fact, the two were so close that there were rumours of a romantic relationship between them.

Barry and Somerset survived the scandal, and in 1827

James Barry 1792-1795–1865

Barry was promoted to staff surgeon and posted to Mauritius, a small island in the Indian Ocean. When he left South Africa, he took along two companions, Dantzen, a black servant who stayed with Barry until he died, and Psyche, one of a series of white dogs he would own during his lifetime. Over the next two decades, other postings and promotions took him to St. Helena, the island where Napoleon had died, then to Jamaica, Trinidad, the Windward and Leeward Islands, Malta, and Corfu.

Barry seemed to enjoy his nomadic life, even though he

suffered from the heat in the tropics. He was not a wealthy man, so he probably could not have afforded world travel if he had not joined the military.

When the Crimean War began in 1853, Barry immediately offered his services. He was turned down, likely because he was considered a troublemaker, but he did persuade his superiors to send soldiers to his hospital on the Greek island of Corfu. As the war progressed, Barry hoped for an appointment as senior medical officer of the Barrack Hospital in Scutari, a section of Istanbul where many Crimean soldiers were sent. He waited for the transfer for two years, but it didn't come through. So he visited Scutari while on leave in 1855 and immediately volunteered his services.

While in Scutari, he met Florence Nightingale, the pioneer British nurse who was one of the most famous women of the time. By now, Barry was close to 60, but his energy and aggressive attitude had not diminished. Nightingale, who was then in her early 30s, did not like Barry any more than he liked her. Both were determinedly outspoken in their crusades to get the best treatment possible for the soldiers in their care, and frequently offended people with their sharp tongues. Probably because they were so much alike, they often clashed.

One of their conflicts resulted in public humiliation for the young nurse. Whatever the specifics of their conflict, Nightingale was furious with the way Barry treated her and wrote angrily to her sister that he had given her the worst scolding she had ever received. According to Nightingale's letter, Barry was seated on horseback when he stopped her as she was crossing the Hospital Square on foot. It was hot, and, lacking a parasol, Nightingale had only a cap to protect her from the sun.

> *He kept me standing in the midst of quite a crowd of soldiers, Commissariat, servants, camp followers, etc., etc., every one of whom behaved like a gentleman during the scolding I received while he behaved like a brute.*

Barry had always been outspoken and forceful, but by this time he was impatient, irascible, and querulous. This behaviour was partly the result of various health problems, including recurring bouts of yellow fever.

After the Crimean War ended, Barry stayed in Corfu for a few months then took an extended leave in England in 1857. While there, he learned that his next posting would be in Canada.

Considering that Barry had spent his entire career in warmer countries and was an acknowledged expert on tropical diseases, the new posting did not seem to make much sense. Presumably, his difficult personality contributed to the decision to send him to Canada, which was still considered something of a backwater. Although Montreal was the largest and most cosmopolitan city in the United Province of Canada in the 1850s, it could not compare to London,

England, which Barry had so recently left. Still, Montreal was the financial and administrative centre of Canada and attracted some interesting and powerful people, so there were compensations. More importantly, the new posting came with a promotion — Barry was appointed local inspector of hospitals for the British Army. In that capacity, he was in charge of overseeing the operation of military hospitals and barracks in Quebec City, Montreal, Kingston, and Toronto.

He threw himself into his work with characteristic zeal. Despite his infirmities, including chronic bronchitis that was made worse by cold Montreal winters, Barry still had enormous energy.

He immediately started pushing for changes that would make soldiers' lives better. Streams of memos and reports urged changes of various kinds, such as improvements in the terrible sewer and drainage conditions at the Quebec barracks. He also insisted that military hospitals replace their vermin-infested straw-stuffed pillows and mattresses with bedding filled with either hair or feathers. Further, he was convinced that the soldier's daily ration of one pound of meat and one pound of bread was inadequate, so he ordered larger quantities of both, as well as vegetables. In addition, to provide a change from a steady diet of boiled beef and soup, he had ovens installed in all barracks cookhouses so the cooks could roast meat and bake bread.

His concerns were not only for the soldiers, however. Barry had long been interested in women's issues. As a medical student in Edinburgh, Scotland, he had studied midwifery and other subjects relating to women's health. In 1826, he had performed the first successful Caesarean section in Africa, and one of the first in the world. Once he had settled into his new job, he focused on one of the problems faced by soldiers' wives, namely the complete lack of privacy.

Married couples were billeted in the general barracks, along with single men. As he wrote in an official report, for "a woman humbly born, but modestly and religiously educated," this was a shocking situation.

> *She becomes frightened or disgusted, next becomes habituated, or in despair has recourse to drunkenness, and not infrequently the husband, a good man, joins with his wife and he becomes the occupant of a cell in a military prison.*

Although work and his many reform campaigns occupied much of Barry's time, he also found enough energy to socialize. Some younger acquaintances found him a bit boring, but there were plenty of others who liked and admired him. When a private gentleman's club — the St. James — was established in Montreal in July 1857, Barry was one of the charter members.

Throughout the winter of 1857–58, Barry was frequently seen along the streets of Montreal as he raced from one duty to another. He rode in a bright red sleigh, often accompanied by Dantzen and Psyche. They were a distinctive and rather eccentric-looking trio — the burly black man, the small white dog, and the frail doctor. Although Barry invariably dressed in his army uniform, complete with a peaked cap with gold braid, he hardly looked impressive. He was now over sixty, and so frail that he seemed almost to disappear into his great coat.

Even though the weather aggravated his chronic bronchitis, military authorities insisted he spend another winter in Montreal. But by 1859, Barry's health had deteriorated to the point that he was forced him to return to England.

Soon after his arrival, he was summoned to a military medical board, which determined that he was no longer fit for duty. He was put on half-pay, and virtually retired from service. Barry, who had never managed to save enough money for retirement, objected strenuously. He sought help from friends and acquaintances and protested to medical authorities, but was unable to secure another posting. Over the next few years, he grudgingly accepted his situation and spent his time visiting friends in Britain. Around 1860, he paid a farewell visit to Jamaica, with his black manservant and dog still at his side.

In the summer of 1865, while Barry was staying in London, the metropolis was hit with a heat wave. Time and again throughout his career, Barry had dealt with the lethal combinations of summer heat, crowded towns, and poor sanitation, which fostered deadly diseases. Now, Barry himself was felled by these conditions. He fell ill with chronic diarrhoea. At 70, and already ailing, he was unable to fight off the condition. At 4 o'clock on the morning of July 25, 1865, Dr. James Barry died at 14 Margaret Street, Cavendish Square, Marleybone, England.

Barry's manservant summoned Sophia Bishop, one of the household servants, to prepare the body for burial. While she washed and arranged the body, military authorities were informed. Major Dr. McKinnon, Barry's physician, signed the death certificate, which Sophia witnessed. Because she was illiterate, Sophia marked the document with an *X*.

And there matters might have ended, with James Barry and his career slowly fading into obscurity, if not for the doctor's miserly landlady.

In early August, Sophia called at the offices of the army agents who were handling Dr. Barry's estate. She was angry. The woman she worked for — the landlady — had refused to pay her for laying out the doctor. They had quarrelled and Sophia had stomped out of the house. It seemed to Sophia that the army should be able to compensate her, and, if they wanted proof that she had done her job, all they needed to do was contact the man who signed the death certificate, Dr. McKinnon.

McKinnon was duly summoned, and the woman angrily explained her situation. She ended with a statement she felt would prove that she had, without a doubt, laid out the doctor. Her observation would scandalize much of the English-speaking world.

"Dr. Barry was a female," she said vehemently, and added that McKinnon was "a pretty doctor not to know it."

The doctor responded, equally angrily, that it was none of her business whether Dr. Barry was a male or a female. He added that, in his opinion, Barry had been neither completely male nor completely female, but "an imperfectly developed man."

Although the woman must have been shocked by this reply, she was not about to let the matter rest. She insisted that she had examined the body, and that it was a perfect female. She backed up this claim by telling McKinnon that marks on the cadaver's body proved Barry had given birth when she was very young.

McKinnon asked for more details, and carefully noted Sophia's answer in his report to the Registrar General. "The woman, pointing to the lower part of her stomach, said 'from marks here ... I am a married woman and the mother of nine children and I ought to know.'" For Sophia, stretch marks were the ultimate proof that she was right.

Within two weeks, the story hit the British newspapers. On August 21, the *Manchester Guardian* ran a brief report of the "incredible" story. After summarizing Barry's career, the report stated,

> *It stands as an indubitable fact, that a woman was for 40 years an officer in the British service, and fought one duel and had sought many more, had pursued a legitimate medical educa-*

tion, and received a regular diploma, and had acquired almost a celebrity for skill as a surgical operator!

Almost anyone who had ever encountered Barry reflected on what they knew about him. They recalled that as a young doctor in Cape Town, he had been a dashing figure, something of a dandy, who was always fashionably dressed, carried a long sword, flirted with women, and was more than willing to fight duels.

In hindsight, many people commented on his short stature, small hands, hairless cheeks, and high-pitched voice. But set against this was his forcefulness and outstanding abilities as a doctor, administrator, and reformer. In a time when women were considered to be intellectually inferior to men, it seemed impossible that a mere female could have been a competent military doctor *and* fooled everyone for more than 40 years!

But had they been fooled? Over the next several years, snippets of information emerged that suggested some people either knew or had guessed at Barry's secret.

Writing to Registrar General George Graham, Dr. McKinnon stated that he had been friends with Barry for years and had attended him in his final illness, and it was his opinion that Barry was a hermaphrodite, a person with both male and female sex organs.

Dr. G. W. Campbell, who had cared for Barry when he was sick with bronchitis in Montreal, stated that Barry's room was always very dark when he called and he had never examined his patient closely enough to make an informed decision one way or another.

Another story claimed that, while Barry was severely ill and unconscious in Trinidad, a doctor had gone to his room to examine him. On removing the bed sheets, he saw that Barry was a woman. But, after his patient regained consciousness, agreed to keep the secret.

At least two other people told dramatic stories of how furious Barry became when they entered his room unannounced. The speculation continued for years, but without any solid scientific evidence, it remained just that, speculation.

Nor was Barry's sex the only mystery. There was little information about his origins — no birth certificate, no childhood acquaintances to shed some light on his early years. There were rumours that he was somehow related to powerful British aristocrats, but again, there was no solid proof. And so Dr. James Barry's reputation as a brilliant medical man and social reformer was overshadowed by fictional or lavishly embellished accounts of his life put out by people who hardly knew him.

This mystery has intrigued people for more than a century. In 2002, Rachel Holmes published a biography, *Scanty Particulars*, which presented a persuasive case that Dr. James Barry was raised as a girl, Margaret, at least until adolescence.

Holmes theorized that Barry had appeared to be a girl until a testicle descended some time in adolescence. This, of course, precluded marriage. Because Margaret's mother, Mary Anne Bulkley, had little money, the teenager had to find some other means of support. Since few careers were open to women in the early 19th century, the obvious choice was for Margaret to pose as a young man. Thus, Margaret Bulkley became James Barry, who, with the financial help of an uncle, James Barry, RA, went to university and became a doctor.

Margaret's reincarnation as James Barry is supported by two facts. A letter Margaret wrote to her uncle shows handwriting remarkably similar to the doctor's. And, just around the time young James Barry RA moved to Edinburgh, where he lived with his "aunt" Mary Anne Bulkley, Margaret Bulkley vanished from the public record without a trace.

So, did James Barry start life as Margaret Bulkley? There is no absolute answer to that. However, his attitude to women makes it seem likely. Throughout his long career, Dr. Barry showed a sympathy for women and women's issues that was highly unusual for the times in which he lived. This extraordinary viewpoint, added to his intelligence and tenacity, made him an effective physician. Whether this physician was an effeminate male, a woman masquerading as a man, or a hermaphrodite who chose a male identity is an intriguing but, ultimately, unimportant aspect in an interesting and worthwhile life.

Chapter 3

The Performer: William Townsend

William Townsend was one bad dude. Although there was little in his background to account for his lawlessness, he seems to have taken to it naturally.

He was born in Black Rock (Buffalo), New York, on August 7, 1832, the son of a carpenter and joiner. While William was growing up, the family moved to Port Dalhousie, near St. Catharines, Ontario, then went to live on a farm close to Canfield, in Haldimand County.

By the time Townsend reached his teens, his father had died and he was forced to support himself. Like many young men of the time, Townsend held a variety of jobs. At 15, he signed aboard the *Mohawk*, a government boat. He immersed himself in sailors' culture, even having his ears pierced and his wrists tattooed — one with an anchor, the other with his initials, W. T. But he soon got into mischief. Some time in 1848, he sold the *Mohawk*'s small boat to someone in Dunnville for $5. And then he deserted the ship.

He drifted from job to job, sometimes working on barges

and boats along the Welland Canal, other times working on farms. For a little while he worked at a sawmill in North Cayuga Township. Yet even while he was working there, he was looking for an easier way to make a living. One of the owners, Reverend Mr. Haw, was expecting a large payment of cash. When Townsend began asking questions about the money, Haw warned his family to keep their eyes and ears open. William Townsend already had a rather unsavoury reputation.

Around 1851, Townsend decided to acquire a trade and tried coopering. But after he was hired — and quickly fired — by two or three barrel makers in Dunnville, he turned to general labour. Then, for a while, he drove a cab in Hamilton. But none of the jobs lasted because, long before he was an adult, William Townsend had learned that there were other, more enjoyable ways to make money.

Townsend was an agile acrobat, a passable actor, and could play several instruments. He was also a talented mimic. He could imitate almost any accent he heard and was also an excellent female impersonator. It was said he sometimes convinced people that he was his own sister, whom he closely resembled. Given these skills — and the fact that he seemed unable to hold down a regular job — he decided to become a travelling performer.

With some other young men, all in their late teens and early twenties, he formed a travelling troupe that put on black-face minstrel shows and other entertainment. Townsend played the tunes of the day on his violin, tambourine, and even the bones (similar to castanets), and acted any part demanded of him. The troupe toured across a wide area of southern Ontario, from the Niagara Peninsula to London, playing at fairs and other special events. It was not a particularly easy way to earn a living, even if Townsend enjoyed performing. However, entertaining may not have been his first priority. As travelling players, he and his companions had the perfect cover for an assortment of crimes, including picking pockets.

By 1854, Townsend and some of his cronies were well known to authorities. That October, they played at the London fair. On their journey back to familiar territory, they moved east along what is now Highway 3, through Norfolk County and into Haldimand County. Dropping all pretence of being showmen, they turned to robbery.

They stopped at general stores, brandishing pistols and demanding cash. In one store, one member of the gang grabbed the owner by the hair and pulled him across the counter, while another gang member took cash from the till. They even became highwaymen, waving down farmers driving their teams along the road. The gang demanded money then cut the reins on the wagons so their victims could not follow them easily.

On the night of Wednesday, October 18, Townsend, along with John Blowes, George King, William Bryson, and John Lettice, reached Nelles' Corners, a small crossroads community west of Cayuga, Haldimand's county town. They decided to rob the combined home and store of John Hamilton Nelles. Darkness had fallen and the entire household was in bed when William Townsend pounded on the front door and demanded to be let in. There was no response. Townsend repeated his demand, shouting, "Open the door or I'll blow you through." The terrified occupants leapt from their beds and John Nelles tried to bar the door. But he was no match for the ruffians, who soon pushed their way in. Moments later, three shots rang out. John Nelles staggered back and collapsed on the carpet.

Augustus Nelles, John's brother, later reported that three men had entered the house. Two wore black hats, but the man who pulled the trigger — who was also the tallest and obviously the leader — wore a white cap. His hair, which was parted in the middle under the cap, was long, curled, and carefully oiled. He was wearing earrings, and his face was half-hidden by a dark beard and a moustache. Augustus thought the whiskers were fake.

John's wife and his sister-in-law, Lucy Humphrey, emerged from the bedroom, one of them holding an infant. When the intruders demanded money, Mrs. Nelles pointed towards the bedroom. As the four men moved in that direction, she scrambled out a window and ran to a neighbour for help. Lucy tried to follow, but before she could reach the window, one of the men came back into the room. Five minutes later, the Townsend gang was on the road with their loot — one gold watch.

A doctor was summoned but there was nothing he could do to save John Nelles. Three bullets had entered the left side of his chest. He lingered until midnight, complaining of pains in his back, then died.

Meanwhile, William Townsend had removed his false beard and moustache. He and his gang headed for Cayuga, where they stopped at a tavern. There, one of the gang persuaded the owner, George Gibson, to drive them to the train station at Canfield. After spending several hours in the Canfield hotel, they boarded the eastbound train at 4 a.m. Soon after daybreak on October 19, they were in Buffalo, New York.

Word of the robbery and murder reached Cayuga around 8 a.m. Peter Campbell, high constable of Haldimand County, asked for volunteers to form a posse. He chose five, presumably because they knew some of the gang members. When they reached the train station in Canfield, a sixth man joined them. He was Robert Flanders, a man who had known William Townsend for some time. The group caught the first available train for Buffalo, arriving about 4 p.m.

By this time, the Buffalo police had been alerted by telegram and had placed observers at every wharf and railroad station. They soon turned up a lead: gang members had been seen at the U.S. Hotel at 3 p.m. Unfortunately, they were gone by the time the police arrived. For the next several hours, lawmen searched every hotel and bar in the city without success.

Meanwhile, the gang had split up. Three of them headed for the Hamilton area, while Townsend and John Lettice made their way to Niagara Falls. Late Saturday, October 21, or early Sunday, October 22, Canadian authorities were told that Townsend and Lettice were in Pelham Township, west of Niagara Falls. Enlisting the help of several locals, the posse tracked them to a 10-acre patch of woods. The men were split into smaller groups and posted in different areas around the woods, waiting for Townsend and Lettice to emerge. But when they finally appeared, Townsend had a pistol in each hand. He told the two men patrolling that spot to leave him alone or he would shoot. They took him at his word, and the desperadoes made their escape.

Soon afterwards, the fugitives parted company. Townsend hurried to St. Catharines. After trading the watch he had stolen from Nelles for a fur coat and heavy gloves, he boarded the *Westchester*, a sailing ship bound for Oswego, New York.

Robert Flanders picked up Townsend's trail a few hours later. After talking to some sailors, he learned that the easterly winds blowing on Lake Ontario would slow the *Westchester* considerably. So Flanders rushed to Niagara-on-the-Lake, where he caught a steamship bound for Oswego.

It looked as though Townsend was trapped. Flanders arrived long before the *Westchester* slipped into port. When it finally docked, the lawman eyed every crewman and passenger and examined every bale and barrel of goods on board — despite the captain's annoyance.

To Flanders' consternation, Townsend was not on board. Seemingly, he had vanished into thin air. Flanders lingered in Oswego hoping to uncover another clue before the trail went completely cold. Not until that evening, several hours after the *Westchester* had docked, did he learn the truth. Over a plate of oysters, the captain informed him that a fellow answering Townsend's description had indeed boarded his vessel in St. Catharines. A short time later, in the nearby harbour of Port Dalhousie, the *Westchester* passed close to a ship heading for Kingston. The young man abruptly jumped from the *Westchester* to the second vessel. The daring leap was completely in character for Townsend. He was fit and agile, accustomed to turning somersaults and performing other stunts for his audiences. Once again, he had eluded his pursuers.

Although friends of John Nelles offered a $100 reward for the capture of the murderers, little initial progress was made. On October 21, three days after the murder, a fellow named Garrett Patterson was arrested in Hamilton. He was a known associate of Townsend and was suspected of participating in the Nelles robbery. But Patterson had an alibi — several people had seen him elsewhere at the time of the crime — so he was soon freed.

Then, in December, the three gang members who had parted company with Townsend and Lettice the day after the murder were apprehended. First, Blowes was caught in

Hamilton. A short time later, George King was captured in Saltfleet Township, east of the city. The third man, William Bryson, was soon in custody.

Meanwhile, Townsend had made his way back to the Niagara Peninsula, where his brother-in-law sheltered him for nearly two months. During that time, his younger sister, Frances, visited him at least once. So did his mother. It was later rumoured that Townsend escaped detection for so long because he usually disguised himself as a woman.

Still, he was not the type of man to sit still for long. He went out frequently, sometimes wearing his false whiskers. In early December — probably because he was desperate for money — he robbed a farmer in the vicinity of Port Robinson, on the Welland Canal. The farmer alerted Constable Charles Richards, who trailed Townsend to an inn owned by a certain widow Jordan. Richards, probably thinking of collecting the reward money, waited alone until Townsend came out of the house then seized him. Townsend struggled, shouting that he had a pistol and would kill Richards if he didn't let go. Richards held on, but not tightly enough. Townsend pulled his gun from his pocket and shot the constable point-blank in the forehead.

Realizing that he had little chance of staying at large for long in the Niagara Peninsula, Townsend headed west. He took the train to Woodstock, 80 kilometres northwest of Cayuga, but by the time he arrived, authorities had been alerted to the second murder. When the train pulled into the station, three or four constables were waiting to search the train.

George Forbes, the Oxford county jailer who had been deputized for the occasion, realized instantly that a young man in one of the cars fit the description of the wanted man. But he was surprised by the passenger's reaction to his careful scrutiny. "Oh! I know what you are at. You take me to be Townsend."

"Yes I do," the constable responded.

"Oh," said the young man, "I do favour the description very much; I have been taken for him once before to-day, but I'm not he. I am going west, and come from the east of Rochester."

The constable later remarked, "He was so well dressed and had such a smile on his face that I did not arrest him. I went to take counsel with the other constables and when I went into the car again he was gone."

But the young man had not gone far — he was standing quietly on the station platform. The lawmen immediately surrounded him and accused him of being the murderer. He remained quiet and cooperative, insisting he was innocent and claiming that friends, who were aboard the next train, could identify him. He was so convincing that the constables did not make any effort to restrain him. Then the train on which he had been riding started to pull out of the station. The little knot of men stood very still as it passed. Just as the train "had attained a good rate of speed, he darted away like a deer and jumped on the last platform of the last car, leaving us behind."

That was the last time Townsend was seen for several months.

On April 13, 1855, the gang members who had been captured — Bryson, Blowes, and King — went on trial at the Haldimand County courthouse in Cayuga. As expected, all three were found guilty and sentenced to hang. Hundreds of people streamed into Cayuga on May 18 to watch the execution. The gallows were set up in front of the courthouse, in full view of the public. But only two prisoners mounted the scaffold that day. Because of his youth, and because he had not entered the Nelles store, William Bryson's sentence was commuted to a prison term in Kingston Penitentiary.

The executions gave the community some assurance that justice had been done, but Lettice and Townsend were still at large. According to local legend, Lettice was killed during a robbery a short time after the execution. As late as July 1855, however, no trace of William Townsend could be found.

Finally, in August 1855, a report reached Haldimand County authorities that a man fitting Townsend's description had been located in Rock Island, in western Illinois. Robert Flanders, the Canfield man who had pursued Townsend the previous autumn, was still a part-time constable. Since he could identify Townsend, he was sent to take him into custody.

Townsend was again involved in the entertainment business, this time with a travelling sideshow. When Flanders caught up with the show he discreetly told the owner that one of his employees was wanted for murder. Before the U.S. authorities could make an arrest, the troupe moved on. Doggedly, Flanders stayed on their trail, but once more was disappointed. The circus owner had told the ringmaster about Flanders' mission. When the ringmaster warned Townsend, the fugitive disappeared again.

Almost two years passed before Townsend resurfaced. In April 1857, Arthur Knowlton, a conductor on the Columbus and Cleveland Railway, approached a dozing passenger who was travelling to Cleveland. The young man — who appeared to be in his mid-twenties — had no money to cover the $3.50 fare, so Knowlton took his pistol, explaining that he knew an innkeeper who would lend him the fare if the pistol was left as security.

Once they reached their destination, the conductor escorted the passenger to a tavern kept by John Iles, who had moved to Cleveland from Haldimand County less than a year earlier. Iles was washing glasses when the pair arrived. When he caught sight of the young man, he dropped one of the heavy tumblers, smashing it to pieces. Unless his eyes were deceiving him, the man was William Townsend!

Recovering his composure, he took the young man's gun as security, paid his debt, then told him to sit down and eat. As soon as his back was turned, Iles hid the weapon then ran to get the police. Moments later, William Townsend was arrested for the murders of John Nelles and Charles Richards. When he tried to escape, the police handcuffed him.

Townsend was transported to the Haldimand County jail in Cayuga, where he waited for several months. At some point during this period, he stated that he was not William Townsend at all, but a Scottish sailor, Robert J. McHenry. Townsend's lawyer, S. B. Freeman of Hamilton, based his defence on the issue of the prisoner's identity. But he was up against tough competition. The outcome of the case was considered so important that Canadian Solicitor General Henry Smith served as Crown prosecutor.

The man accused of murdering John Hamilton Nelles went on trial on Thursday, September 24, 1857. Through Thursday, Friday, and part of Saturday, dozens of witnesses took the stand. According to one local newspaper, Caledonia's *Grand River Sachem*, "There were 36 witnesses for the Crown, most of whom swore *positively* to Townsend's identity, and 54 for the defence, who were equally *positive* that he was not that notorious rascal."

Photography was in its infancy, fingerprinting unheard of. Establishing the prisoner's identity depended on the credibility of witnesses whose motives and powers of observation varied considerably. Depending on who was on the stand, Townsend's eyes were either dark or hazel. The man who called himself McHenry had blue eyes. Townsend's hair was dark, straight, and low on his forehead. "McHenry's" was lighter, and his forehead was quite prominent. Townsend's eyebrows met over his nose. "McHenry's" did not. Townsend's voice was high-pitched and nasal. "McHenry's" voice was lower and he had a pronounced Scottish accent.

Then there were the matters of the scars and distinguishing marks. Townsend's wrists had been tattooed, and, according to one witness, he also had a mermaid on one arm. "McHenry" had no such marks — although some evidence was given that tattoos, which were probably self-applied, could be removed. More than one witness mentioned a scar on Townsend's face. "McHenry" also had a scar, but it was only visible after the first day of the trial, when he had been shaved on the order of the court.

The prisoner's feet also attracted a lot of attention. Burton Wait, a man who had once compared scars with Townsend, described a scar that started at the joint of his great toe and ran around to the ball of his foot. When the accused was ordered to remove his boot, the scar was there for all to see. This piece of "proof" might have swayed some of the jury, but other witnesses, including William Townsend's mother, cast doubt on its value. Mrs. Townsend, who repeatedly denied the prisoner was her son, testified that William Townsend had large toe joints, which were obvious even when wearing boots. Another witness, Benjamin Diffin, backed up this fact. Diffin, a cooper for whom Townsend had worked one winter, described the foot problem in some detail. He even related a scenario in which Townsend tried but failed to wear his employer's boots. When Diffin looked at the feet of the accused, he said they were smaller than Townsend's. Then the prisoner was ordered to try on Diffin's boots. They slid on easily.

The man who claimed to be McHenry hampered his defence by refusing to fill in many gaps in his past. He did provide a detailed description of Springburn, a village near Glasgow, Scotland, which rang true with several people. However, the Crown Attorney quickly pointed out that Townsend's stepfather, David Dewar, was from Scotland and could have described the village to the accused. Furthermore, he reminded the court, Townsend was well-known for his ability to imitate a Scottish accent. When Dewar took the stand, he testified that he came from Fifeshire, 50 or 60 miles distant from Glasgow, and insisted that he had never described any part of Scotland to his stepson.

Confusing matters still further was the motivation of the witnesses. As the Crown pointed out, many of the defence witnesses were Townsend's relatives, or individuals of dubious background who might be expected to assist him in evading justice.

The defence countered that some of the Crown witnesses had their own agenda. They pointed out that John Iles, the man who had summoned police to make the arrest in Cleveland, had previously turned in another man in order to collect reward money. And William Bryson, the gang member whose death sentence had been commuted to life in prison, might have identified the accused as Townsend in hopes of getting a shorter jail term.

In the end, the jury could not make up its mind. After more than six hours of deliberation, from 3:30 Saturday after-noon until 10 that night, they informed the judge that seven were convinced the man was Townsend, four swore he was not, and one was undecided. Without a unanimous verdict, the judge had no choice but to thank the jury and let them go. But there was no immediate freedom for the accused. He now had to stand trial for the murder of Constable Richards in Port Robinson.

The second trial took place in Welland in April 1858. Again, the main issue was the identity of the accused, but this time there was a new twist. Four men testified that the man in the prisoner's dock was McHenry and that he had been mining in Chip's Flats, California, around the time of the Nelles murder. Therefore he could not possibly be William Townsend and he could not have killed Constable Richards. Along with other testimony, which was similar to that given in Cayuga, this was enough to convince the jury that the wrong man was being tried. The accused, now being addressed as Bob McHenry, was set free.

But was he really Robert J. McHenry? One of the ques-tions the prosecution had asked at the first trial was why an innocent man would have languished in jail for six months if he could have provided an alibi. The accused replied that, in fact, he had taken steps to provide an alibi within a few weeks of reaching the Haldimand County jail. On June 29, 1857, he had arranged for a letter to be sent to the secretary of the Sons of Temperance in California. Apparently, he had once been a member of the organization and hoped some of his fellow members would come to his aid. But, it would have taken several weeks for the message to reach its destination and several more weeks before any witnesses could arrive in southern Ontario.

Were the witnesses who swore that the accused was McHenry telling the truth when they said they had known McHenry in California *and that he had been there at the time of the Nelles murder*? Two were Canadians who had returned home before the second trial. Another was living in New York State. It is quite possible that they knew William Townsend and were willing to provide him with both a new identity and an alibi.

At least one writer has suggested that the man tried in Cayuga and Welland was neither William Townsend nor Robert McHenry but a third man, possibly a deserter from the British army, who had his own reasons for keeping quiet about much of his past.

That is certainly possible, but it is also possible that the man on trial was, indeed, William Townsend. Recent scientific studies have proven that eyewitnesses, even with the best intentions in the world, often misremember or misinterpret what they have seen. That possibility, along with the desire of many of the witnesses to protect William Townsend, may have been enough to create an element of doubt in the minds of the jurors.

What may have ultimately tipped the scale was the behaviour of the accused. Although Bryson testified that the prisoner swore loudly when he identified him in his cell, McHenry's behaviour in the courtroom was extremely cool. He cooperated fully, showing his scars or removing his boots when asked. He was so unruffled that he even read newspapers when he found the proceedings too tedious.

Were these the actions of an innocent man, one who was convinced he would ultimately be acquitted? Or was William Townsend — thief, murderer, musician, and mimic — giving the best performance of his life? We shall probably never know. Neither William Townsend nor Robert J. McHenry was ever heard of again.

Chapter 4

The Millionaire's Daughter: Cassie Chadwick

D r. Leroy Chadwick of Cleveland, Ohio, took a desperate step. Recently widowed, the wealthy doctor sorely missed female companionship, and so he decided to visit a well-known house of prostitution. That evening in the mid-1890s would become a turning point in his life.

He was greeted at the door by a young woman and told to wait while his presence was announced. The young woman advised Mrs. Cassie L. Hoover, the brothel's madam, of his presence, noting that he was a doctor and obviously rich. In a matter of moments, Mrs. Hoover planned her strategy. Toning down her normally flashy costume for something more respectable, she went downstairs to meet the doctor.

No one could call her beautiful, but with carefully coiffed hair and a smooth oval face, she was certainly attractive for a woman in her late thirties. Cassie was fashionably plump, but her mouth was delicate, her eyebrows finely

Cassie L. Chadwick, 1857-1907

arched. True, her nose was rather large and blunt, and when she frowned she looked very grim. But she was not frowning now. Fixing her large, dark eyes on Dr. Chadwick, she turned on the charm.

After a short conversation, it became clear that Dr. Chadwick was not in the habit of visiting prostitutes and that he was gullible. Cassie decided to test that gullibility — a quality she admired in a man.

She explained that she was also a widow, forced by economic circumstances to seek work. It was her first day on the job as manager of the place — a girls' boarding house —

but she was not certain she had made the right choice. The young women in her custody seemed to come and go with alarming frequency, and their behaviour was not as respectable as she would have wished. However, she understood that modern young women, especially those who needed to work for a living, were not always as genteel as one would desire.

Dr. Chadwick looked at her in amazement. Did she not realize, he asked, that the boarding house was actually one of the better-known houses of ill repute in the city? No, she did not, Mrs. Hoover replied, then fainted dead away. When she regained consciousness, Dr. Chadwick had loosened her collar and was chafing her wrists, a look of concern on his face. As soon as she came to her senses, Mrs. Hoover recalled his startling revelation. Horrified, she begged the good doctor to take her out of the place immediately.

Touched by the widow's plight, Dr. Chadwick complied. There was no question of taking her to a hotel at that late hour as he was known in Cleveland and it would have caused too much gossip. Instead, he offered Mrs. Hoover the hospitality of his home on Euclid Avenue, part of Cleveland's "Millionaire's Row." She gratefully accepted. Less than a year later Cassie and Dr. Chadwick were married.

Cassie and Leroy were about the same age but their backgrounds could not have been more dissimilar. He was well known in Cleveland society, just as his first wife had been. Cassie, on the other hand, was a bit of a mystery —

even to her new husband. As the months passed, however, he learned more and more about her, including her expectation of eventually inheriting a fortune and that she had a young son, Emil.

One of the first things he learned about Cassie was that she seemed to have a better head for business than he did. Realizing he was not particularly skilled in matters of finance, he allowed her to take over the management of his money and real estate holdings. He may have begun to regret this decision quite early on, for Cassie proved to be a woman of extravagant tastes. She dressed lavishly, often draping herself in furs. She also had a passion for diamonds, which she was rumoured to buy by the tray. But her extravagance didn't stop there. She filled their home with opulent furniture and ornaments, many of which were not to the doctor's taste. One December evening, Cassie surpassed herself. While Leroy was at the opera, she had the house extensively redecorated as a Christmas surprise.

Many rich Victorians liked to display their wealth with stately mansions, rich decoration, and plush furniture, but the new Mrs. Chadwick was considered ostentatious to the point of vulgarity. This, as well as her evident lack of good breeding, did not endear her to her husband's social set. Neighbours and colleagues accepted invitations to the Chadwick home after Cassie and Leroy married, and, as a matter of course, reciprocated. Then the invitations dwindled. As one newspaper article explained, Cassie never

The Millionaire's Daughter: Cassie Chadwick

really belonged to Cleveland society. "The social path of Mrs. Chadwick has been stormy, her efforts to break into the exclusive set have not been crowned with great success."

Cassie made matters worse for herself by trying to buy acceptance. She purchased extravagant presents for acquaintances, including, on one memorable occasion, pianos for eight young women. Another time, she hired a private railway car and took a party of people to New York to see an opera. Then, in the fall of 1898, she took twelve young society women on a European tour and showered them with gifts.

When she returned to Cleveland, she realized that she had spent most of her husband's fortune. Leroy apparently had no clue about his precarious financial position, and Cassie was determined to keep it hidden from him. She was a resourceful woman who had been faced with money problems before. It wasn't long before she formulated a plan that would allow her to continue her sumptuous style of living.

She visited Oberlin, a city southwest of Cleveland, and called on Charles B. Beckwith, the president of the Citizens' National Bank. She told him that she wanted to make a sizeable donation to Oberlin College, but all her funds were currently tied up. The respectable Mrs. Cassie Chadwick then asked if it would be possible for the bank to lend her the money for a short term. Beckwith explained he could not lend her any of the bank's money, but Cassie was not a woman to take no for an answer. She was so charming and persuasive that he finally offered to advance her a sum from his own account.

Then Cassie dropped her bombshell. She also had a promissory note in her bag, signed by her father. Feigning embarrassment, she poured out her story, likely stopping only to dab at her eyes or to steal a look at him.

According to Cassie, her father had been a poor Scottish immigrant who had come to the United States as a boy. He was ambitious and seemed well on his way to a successful career when his girlfriend became pregnant. It was a time when marriage and fatherhood could dramatically slow a young man's progress up the corporate ladder. So her father refused to marry her mother; when Cassie was born she was sent to Ontario, Canada, where she was raised by a kindly family named Bigley. Years passed. Her mother died, having never married, and her father had become enormously wealthy. Regretting his youthful indiscretion, but still careful of his reputation as a respectable businessman, her father contacted her. They were reconciled and he promised that, in time, she would inherit part of his fortune. As a token of good faith, he had even written promissory notes. In fact, Cassie told Beckwith, she had a note for a quarter of a million dollars in her handbag.

Charles Beckwith was astonished by the story, and even more so when he examined the signature on the note. Cassie Chadwick's father was Andrew Carnegie, one of the richest and most famous men in the United States.

Born in Scotland in 1835, Carnegie emigrated with his family in 1848. Starting in the telegraph office of Pennsylvania

Railroad Company, he launched a successful career, first in the railway then in a steel company he established in Pittsburgh in 1872. In 1901, he sold the Carnegie Steel Company to J. P. Morgan and retired. Although fabulously wealthy, Carnegie was a strong believer in philanthropy and donated millions of dollars to universities and libraries. Just about everyone in the United States knew about him and his rise from rags to riches.

Beckwith believed everything Cassie told him. He took the note as security, filled out documents stating that she had assets worth $250,000 on deposit at the bank, and promised to tell no one about her connection with Carnegie. What Beckwith could not have known was that Cassie had already told her husband, as well as at least one neighbour.

Next day, Cassie went home to Cleveland, where she paid a call on Iri Reynolds, secretary-treasurer of the Wade Park Banking Company, to ask for a line of credit. Reynolds was acquainted with the Chadwick family; this and the proof that she had securities at the Oberlin bank were enough assurance for Reynolds. He gave her a $125,000 line of credit.

No doubt congratulating herself on duping the two smaller banks, Cassie then went to New York City and visited the Lincoln National Bank. There, she produced the documents from the Oberlin and Cleveland banks, which indicated that she had $375,000 on deposit. In no time at all, she had another bank account at the Lincoln National. She promptly wrote a cheque for $300,000 and sent it to

Beckwith in Oberlin, along with a letter asking him to deduct the money she owed him and to then deposit the surplus in her account.

It would take several weeks for the management at the three banks to sort out what she had done. Without investing a cent, she had persuaded two banks to provide her with credit totalling $375,000, then used the documents they provided to open a chequing account at a third bank. By promptly reimbursing the Oberlin bank and depositing an additional $50,000, Cassie hoped to reinforce Beckwith's confidence in her. And, by using that deposit for leverage, she could go to other banks and borrow enough to cover her first loan. But to pull it off, she had to move quickly and dispose of any potentially harmful evidence.

She made another visit to Oberlin, where she asked Beckwith to return her promissory note. Her father was angry with her, she explained, because she had revealed his secret. Beckwith was sympathetic, but made it clear he could not return the note until the cheques from Wade Park and Lincoln National had cleared.

Cassie was understanding and not terribly flustered. She had other notes, which she planned to use to her advantage. While on a visit to New York, she met with a lawyer named Dillon, an acquaintance of her husband. On some pretext, she asked him to drive her to Andrew Carnegie's home. While he waited outside, Cassie entered the house. When she emerged, she waved to a man standing in a window. As she entered the carriage, she dropped a piece of paper. Dillon bent to pick it up and discovered it was a promissory note for $2 million, signed by Andrew Carnegie.

Again feigning embarrassment, Cassie explained that she was Carnegie's illegitimate daughter. She begged the lawyer to say nothing about the note, as it would embarrass her father. Delighted to help a charming woman in distress, Dillon offered to put the note in a security box. He also promised to say nothing about Cassie's Carnegie connection.

But Dillon, like many of the other men with whom she had business dealings, could not keep such a juicy piece of gossip to himself. Eventually the secret leaked out, which was just what Cassie had counted on. The little play she had performed in front of Dillon had been classic Cassie. She had actually gone into the Carnegie mansion to see the butler, spinning him a tale of verifying a housemaid's reference.

Drawing on nothing more concrete than a melodramatic story, her considerable charm, and forged promissory notes, Cassie Chadwick maintained her extravagant lifestyle until November 1904. Despite her seemingly sincere pleas for secrecy, several rich and powerful men "knew" that she was Andrew Carnegie's illegitimate daughter. Consequently, they were happy to lend her huge sums of money, secure in the knowledge that Carnegie's fortune would cover Cassie's debts. And, whenever it seemed one of her benefactors was becoming a little uncomfortable with the amount of her debt, Cassie would make a sizeable payment — with borrowed funds.

It was an audacious plan, and for a time Cassie got away with it. But as the months passed, it became more and more difficult to maintain the charade. In a little over four years she had borrowed more than $10 million from businessmen and bankers. Eventually, some of them began asking very pointed questions. In November 1904, everything fell apart. Some of the bankers she had dealt with, including Charles Beckwith, were under investigation.

Cassie fled to a New York City hotel, where the staff protected her as much as possible from aggressive reporters. On December 4, 1904, Charles Beckwith and the Oberlin bank cashier were arrested for violation of federal banking regulations. Beckwith was devastated. He had accepted promissory notes totalling more than $1.25 million from Cassie, a sum that far exceeded the bank's operating capital. In his defence, Beckwith told the investigators that Cassie had sworn the signatures were those of Andrew Carnegie, and that she had seen him sign the notes himself.

> *I am either an awful dupe or a terrible fool. I guess there is no doubt about my being a fool. I know I have done wrong, and although crushed to the earth myself, I do not propose to be made a scapegoat to shield the sins of others. Further concealment of the truth cannot help anyone. The truth is that others also must be called to the bar to answer for their part in this terrible*

*affair, and one of those whose answer must be
had is Mrs. Cassie L. Chadwick.*

As Cassie waited for events to develop, her husband fled
to Europe. Leroy Chadwick claimed to have no knowledge
of his wife's financial activities. He bolstered this claim by
issuing a statement that he had been away in Europe during
much of the time between 1901 and 1904. As a gentleman,
he felt compelled to state that he believed in her innocence.
However, he made no effort to return to the United States as
the scandal unfolded.

Cassie was arrested on the night of December 7. U.S.
Marshals guarded the door of her room as well as the hotel
lobby until the following morning. At 8:45 a.m., she was
escorted from the building and transported to a downtown
office. For several days before the arrest, reports had circulated that she was in a terrible physical state, suffering from
a nervous disorder and possibly in danger of dying. She did
appear rather feeble as she left the hotel, and after climbing
three stories to the U.S. Marshal's office, she fainted. But a
few minutes' rest on a sofa restored her to full health.

The charges were read and she was also identified as
Lydia De Vere, a clairvoyant who had served time for forgery.
Yet, in spite of her record and the charges against her, she was
still able to charm authorities into letting her stay in the relative
comfort of the marshal's office for several hours before being
transferred to a cell in the Tombs, New York City's main jail.

She expected to be out on bail in a very short time, and told reporters that she would be free in two days at the most. However, she did not apply for bail. Possibly, this was on the advice of her lawyer, who may have suggested languishing in a cell was a better strategy than having bail denied. According to newspaper reports, Cassie had "quite regained her remarkable nerve" and "thrown off that tottering gait and trembling weakness." She avidly followed newspaper reports about her case but, naturally, put her own spin on things.

She claimed her husband still had plenty of money and was coming home to support her in her trial. Neither statement was true. She also said, "You may assure my friends and those who believe in me that I will not disappoint the confidence they repose in me. I will show them and the whole world that I am an honest woman." She went on to claim that one of the wealthiest men in the country, who she had known since the age of 12, had offered to post bail but she had chosen to refuse his generous offer.

Meanwhile, the wealthy American that Cassie had claimed to be her father was in the news. Questioned about the notes that Cassie had given out, Andrew Carnegie responded, "Never signed such notes. Have no notes out. Have not issued a note in many years." The multimillionaire was ill at the time and asked if an officer of the court could travel to New York to take his affidavit. Instead, he was subpoenaed.

On December 14, Cassie was transferred from New York to Cleveland. The train was three hours late and by the time it pulled into Cleveland's Union Station, thousands had gathered to see the notorious Mrs. Chadwick. Cassie had anxiously asked her escort to allow the train to stop elsewhere, but this could not be done.

As usual, she was exquisitely dressed in a brown tailored suit and a mauve silk coat. On one arm she carried a brown cape. She also wore a brown hat, to which had been attached an automobile veil. In an attempt to preserve Cassie's privacy, her maid Freda had draped the veil in a double layer, partly obscuring her face.

Freda and Cassie's teenage son Emil led the way, followed by Cassie, who leaned heavily on the arms of two U.S. Marshals. The crowd, largely made up of men and boys, booed, hissed, and jeered as they slowly walked to a waiting carriage. Cassie mustered as much dignity as she could. In her mind, she was a victim of persecution.

Public clamour has "made me a public sacrifice," she told one reporter. "Here I am, an innocent woman, hounded into jail, while a score of the biggest businessmen in Cleveland would leave town tomorrow if I told all that I know. Yes, I borrowed money, but what of it? I will even admit that I did not borrow it in a businesslike way. I wish now that I had followed old rules a little closer. But you can't accuse a poor businesswoman of being a criminal, can you?"

The courts thought differently. Cassie faced several charges, including three of aiding and abetting officers of a national bank to defraud the institutions, and two of conspiring against the United States, which had issued the federal charter for the Citizens' National Bank of Oberlin.

Trial was set for early March. While she waited in the county jail, the Chadwick home was put on the auction block. For several weeks, visitors streamed through the luxurious mansion, gawking at the furniture and accessories that had been purchased partly with stolen funds.

The six-day trial started on March 6. Hundreds of spectators jammed the courtroom, along with a number of witnesses — including Andrew Carnegie. At one recess, he was asked if he would prosecute Cassie when the trial was over. Carnegie responded dryly, "Why should I? Wouldn't you be proud of the fact that your name is good for loans of a million and a quarter dollars, even when someone else signs it? It is glory enough for me that my name is good, even when I don't sign it. Mrs. Chadwick has shown that my credit is A-1."

The outcome was more or less inevitable. Cassie Chadwick was found guilty, and, given her previous record, was sentenced to ten years in jail. In her official prison photograph, Prisoner #36680 looks nothing like the wealthy society matron she had once been. Her grey hair is tightly pulled back in a severe bun, her striped shirtwaist ill-fitting and unfashionable.

Cassie settled into prison life, eating plain food, sleeping on a hard bed, and working at menial tasks in the prison's shirt factory. At night, she likely spent many hours remembering the chequered life that had brought her to this miserable place.

She had been born Elizabeth "Betsy" Bigley near Woodstock, Ontario, in 1857. As a child she was imaginative, often daydreaming and frequently telling lies. In fact, it seemed young Betsy was completely incapable of telling the truth.

According to some accounts, she forged her first cheque at 13. At 22, she was arrested for forgery, but the charges were dismissed on the grounds that she was insane. In 1891, she moved to Cleveland, where she lived with a married sister. One day, while her sister and brother-in-law were away, she mortgaged their furniture to raise some cash. From time to time, Betsy also earned money through prostitution. In 1882, having sold most of her clothes to pay off a loan, she married Dr. Wallace Springsteen. Eleven days later, after learning about her past, he kicked her out of the house. Betsy later demanded $6,000 in support. Springsteen retaliated by accusing her of adultery and producing affidavits from two men. Betsy did not get the money, but Springsteen did pay off all the debts she had incurred during their brief marriage.

After that disastrous relationship, she travelled to Erie, Pennsylvania, and checked into a hotel. Calling herself Maisie, she claimed to be recently widowed and told the hotel owners she wanted to be left alone. They complied for several weeks. Then, just as they began to pressure her for payment, Maisie fell seriously ill. Realizing how bad it would be for business if she died on the premises, they gently persuaded her to leave. A few weeks later, an unsigned letter announced that Maisie had died.

Betsy reinvented herself a few more times. For a while she worked in Cleveland as a clairvoyant, calling herself Madam Lydia De Vere. Telling fortunes did not bring in the kind of money she wanted, so she went back to forging cheques. At some point she also gave birth to Emil, who seems to have been shunted off to friends or relatives whenever Cassie found it convenient.

In 1889, Cassie was arrested, found guilty of forgery, and sentenced to nine-and-a-half years in the Toledo penitentiary. After only three-and-a-half years, she was paroled. She then returned to Cleveland and set herself up as Mrs. Hoover in a west side brothel, which was when Dr. Leroy Chadwick walked into her life.

After years of high living, Cassie found prison difficult, but she was allowed a few luxuries. She had managed to set aside a little money, and some jewels, as well as a number of personal items. Her cell was furnished comfortably, with a rug, a few chairs, and a wardrobe. Several changes of clothes hung inside the wardrobe so that Cassie could look presentable when meeting visitors.

However, her stay in prison was relatively brief. On October 10, 1907, just 19 months after her trial ended, Cassie Chadwick died. She had spent the last months contacting relatives in Ontario and making plans for her funeral, which turned out to be one of the major social events in Woodstock. Cassie would have been most gratified.

Chapter 5
The Secret Agent: Henri Le Caron

I n 1866, without really meaning to, Henri Le Caron launched his 25-year career as a British double agent. It all started with an innocent letter to his father.

Le Caron had recently married and settled in Nashville, Tennessee. Although he was English, he had served in the Union Army during the U.S. Civil War and had attained the rank of major. He continued to use the title after he left the military, and also continued to use the alias he had assumed when joining the army in August 1861: Henri Le Caron.

According to Le Caron's autobiography, the letter home was written in "the careless spirit of a wanderer's notes." Yet it contained information that both intrigued and alarmed his father, John Billis Beach. In particular, the elder Beach was interested in his son's references to John O'Neill, a former brother-in-arms who also happened to be a prominent member of the Irish Republican Brotherhood in the United States.

Beach took the letter to the Liberal member of parliament for Colchester, John Gurdon Rebow. After examining it,

Major Henri Le Caron, 1841-1894

Rebow forwarded it to the Home Office. In a relatively short time, John Beach was writing back to his son in the United States, asking him to provide whatever information he could about Fenian activity.

The letter came at a crossroads in Le Caron's life. He was 25 years old and had just decided to study medicine, but was a happy-go-lucky young man with little thought for the future. His wife's family connections, his military service, and his ambition equipped him for success. Although he was not physically imposing, being small, wiry, and sharp-nosed, he carried himself with the air of a man used to being obeyed and he had a knack for instilling confidence in people. This had not always been the case. During his childhood, his parents had almost given up on him.

Thomas Billis Beach was born in Colchester on September 26, 1841, the son of a Methodist cooper. Beach Sr. and his wife tried to raise their children to be upright, God-fearing citizens, but Thomas was a problem child from the very first.

Unhappy with conditions at home and eager for adventure, he ran away at the age of 12, determined to seek the bright lights of London. On his way out of Colchester, he encountered a school friend, with whom he shared his plan. That proved to be his undoing. In a very short time, his parents caught up with Thomas and took him home. One of the things the young runaway learned from that incident was how to keep secrets.

Before long, he ran away again. This time, he managed to elude his parents for two weeks. When they found him, they brought him home, convinced that he was "the black sheep of the family, from whom no permanent good could ever be expected."

Since he did not seem to have much interest in education, Thomas was then apprenticed to a draper in Colchester. Working with fabrics and living with his "staid and strict" employer was not the boy's idea of a good time.

The apprenticeship ended after 11 months. A short time later, in May 1857, he finally went to London, where he found work through family connections. Again he got into trouble, this time by accidentally setting fire to his employer's premises. He was politely asked to leave. A series of other jobs followed. Then, in 1859, he moved to Paris.

There, he was employed by Arthur & Company, an English banking establishment that specialized in handling U.S. accounts. As a result, young Thomas came into contact with many Americans. When news reached Paris that civil war had broken out in the United States, it was the main topic of conversation among his U.S. acquaintances. Not quite 20, Thomas was quickly caught up in the excitement of doing battle for a noble cause. With several U.S. companions, he sailed for New York and on August 7, 1861, enlisted in the 8th Pennsylvanian Reserves.

At the time of his enlistment, he gave his name as Henri Le Caron, claiming to be a French citizen. In his autobiography, Le Caron explained he did this because his initial term of duty was only three months and he had no plans to stay much longer. Indeed, he "regarded the whole proceeding more in the light of a good joke than anything else." However, because Britain was officially neutral and he did not wish to cause his parents any undue anxiety, he decided to masquerade as a Frenchman. "So came into existence that name and character which, in after years, proved to be such a marvellous source of protection and success to me personally, and of such continued service to my native country."

Le Caron discovered that he liked life in the army, despite the obvious dangers. He enjoyed the comradeship and adventure so much that he stayed in the military until the end of the war — a period of five years. After fighting at Four Oaks, South Mountain, Antietam, and Williamsport, he was relocated with the Western Army to Tennessee. By 1864, he had been promoted to second lieutenant. Throughout the bloody years of the U.S. Civil War, Henri Le Caron survived relatively unscathed.

He had a few close calls, but none as memorable as the events of Christmas Eve 1862. He was scouting with a party of soldiers about 24 kilometres outside of Nashville, and the group stopped at a house to buy some supper. While they were there, the house was surrounded by Confederate marauders. The Confederates captured Le Caron and about half of the Union soldiers who were with him, and imprisoned them in a large log smokehouse. Realizing that their captors were not regular soldiers, the Union men fully believed they were likely to be killed at short notice. They could do nothing but wait and listen to the sounds of their enemies eating and drinking.

After a while, the house became silent. The Confederates had fallen asleep after their feast, as apparently had the guard stationed at the smokehouse door. Then, stealthily, someone drew the bolt from the outside. Nannie Melville, niece of the owner of the house, had lured the guard into the house with the promise of a meal then returned to set the Union soldiers free.

Greatly relieved, Le Caron and his men hiked back to Nashville and safety. The young soldier never forgot the "brave Tennessee girl" who had come to his rescue. Sixteen months later, he met her again in Nashville. Nannie was the daughter of a German woman and a Virginia planter of Irish ancestry, "a bright-eyed daring horsewoman." They began courting, married in 1865, and settled in Nashville.

They were still newlyweds when Le Caron was asked to spy on O'Neill. He does not seem to have spent much time weighing the dangers of a career in espionage. For months he had been hearing about Fenian activities from O'Neill, "at first casually, and in broken conversation." What he learned made him furious, but he had no idea how to stop the subversive activities. Possibly because he realized there was considerable sympathy for the Fenian cause in the United States, he voiced no public criticism of the movement. But his letters to his father apparently made his views clear. Although he had lost his British citizenship upon joining the Union army, when he was asked to spy on O'Neill, Le Caron barely hesitated. He did not even care if he was paid for his efforts. As he later wrote, he was a patriot whose main concern was to help defeat England's enemies.

His main quarry, John O'Neill, was also a patriot — an Irish patriot. Seven years older than Le Caron, O'Neill was born in Ireland but had emigrated to the United States as a teenager. Although O'Neill had been born a British subject, he hated the idea. He wanted to free Ireland from British rule, and in this he was far from alone.

Hunger, economic devastation, and years of political oppression led to a rebellion in 1848. The rebellion failed, but the Irish were undaunted. They were determined to push the English out of their country, and in this they were aided financially by many emigrants who had left for the United States. The U.S. Civil War also helped their cause. When the war began in 1861, the Fenian leadership encouraged their brethren to enlist in order to receive the military training essential for overthrowing British rule. As a result, nearly one in six soldiers in the Union Army was Irish.

Meanwhile, Fenians were also active in Britain. Government authorities in both nations kept a close eye on the organization. When Henri Le Caron's letters came to the attention of the British Home Office, it seemed a made-in-heaven opportunity to spy on Fenian activities.

In April 1866, the Fenians staged their first invasion of Canada. A small group briefly occupied Campobello Island, on the Maine–New Brunswick border. In June, O'Neill led a larger force across the Niagara River and marched on Ridgeway, where they were met by the Canadian militia. On June 7, another group attacked St. Armand, Frelighsburg, and Stanbridge East in the Missisquoi area of Quebec. In each instance, the Fenians were ultimately repelled. Despite the defeats, John O'Neill was determined to attack Canada again.

Le Caron's information was insufficient to stop the first invasion, but authorities were convinced the Fenians would try again. As a result, the young spy continued to work for the British government.

In the fall of 1867, he took a trip back to England to visit his father. While there, he met with some government representatives, and, for the first time, arrangements were made to pay him for his services as a secret agent. His government contacts encouraged him to join the Fenians, which he did on his return to United States. A short time later he arranged a meeting with O'Neill. When the younger man volunteered his services, O'Neill eagerly accepted.

Le Caron continued his medical studies as he became more deeply involved in Fenian affairs. He joined Clan-na-Gael, an offshoot organization. He also organized a Fenian "circle" or branch in Lockport, Illinois, where he had settled with his family. As its "centre," or leader, he received numerous documents from John O'Neill, which he carefully copied and tucked into his letters to his father.

Le Caron's pseudo-friendship with O'Neill paid off in December 1867, when the Irishman was elected president of the organization at the Cleveland Convention. O'Neill's new position was not a complete surprise. He was tall and handsome with a military bearing, a "rich, sonorous voice" and a good deal of charm. But, according to Le Caron, he had one fatal flaw. He was "the most egotistical soul I ever met in the whole course of my life. In his belief, the Irish cause lived, moved, and had its being in John O'Neill." Le Caron was convinced that this characteristic was responsible for many of the Fenians' failures and that a "more even headed leader" might have been more successful.

For the time being, O'Neill was still an impressive leader who kept reminding the Fenians of the need for another invasion of Canada. To accomplish this, the organization decided that military units needed to be put together and drilled. In August 1868, O'Neill summoned Henri Le Caron to New York, telling him his organization needed him. By this time, Le Caron was resident medical officer at the Illinois State Penitentiary. Le Caron dutifully resigned from the penitentiary — even though his boss offered him a raise — and made the trip. In New York, O'Neill appointed him civil organizer for military units in the eastern United States, at a salary of $60 per month, plus expenses of $7 per day.

On the evening Le Caron was appointed to this position, O'Neill insisted that he attend a large rally in Williamsburg, not far from Brooklyn. Several thousand Fenian supporters had turned out to hear a slate of speakers. O'Neill and Le Caron were seated on the platform, one on each side of the chairman, and as each speaker was introduced, O'Neill coached the chairman on what to say. Le Caron waited with growing anxiety, realizing that he would probably be called on to speak. While he could certainly hold his own in conversation or when addressing a small group, he was not an orator. Worse, the only real knowledge he had of Irish politics was what he gleaned through his daily interactions with the Fenians. Le Caron realized there was a very real chance he might be denounced as a spy.

Four or five speakers addressed the multitude and then the moment Le Caron dreaded arrived. The chairman introduced him, but managed to get his name wrong, introducing him as Major "M'Caron." Although his heart was pounding, Le Caron found himself "tickled by the error into which he had fallen, and the vast cheat I was playing on the whole of them." He rose to thunderous applause and addressed the boisterous audience. Le Caron paraphrased his speech in his autobiography.

> *Proud and happy as I was at being with them that evening, and taking part in such a magnificent demonstration, they could not, I said, expect me to detain them long at so advanced an hour. All had been said that could be said upon the subject nearest and dearest to their hearts. (Applause.) If what I had experienced that night was indicative of the spirit of patriotism of the Irish in America — (tremendous cheering) — then indeed there could be no fears for the result. (Renewed plaudits.) And now I would sit down. They were all impatiently waiting, I knew, to hear the stirring words of the gallant hero of Ridgeway, General O'Neill — (thunders*

of applause) — and I would, in conclusion, simply beg of them as lovers of liberty and motherland — (excited cheering) — to place at the disposal of General O'Neill the means (cash) necessary to carry out the great work on which he was engaged.

He ended by expressing his confidence that the Fenians would eventually free Ireland and sat down to the sound of shouts and cheers.

Although Le Caron played up the amusing aspects of the incident, his role as a secret agent was a dangerous one. A few months after his return to the United States in 1867, the identity of another agent was discovered. At one point, the Lord Lieutenant of Ireland and his secretary, the Earl of Mayo, were discussing the agent while dining together at the vice-regal lodge. In the typical fashion of their class, they paid no attention to hovering servants, one of whom repeated the conversation in the servants' quarters. Word eventually reached the Fenians, and the agent was shot soon after he landed in New York.

The assassination had a direct impact on Le Caron. To minimize the risk of discovery, John Beach and the member of parliament who had asked Le Caron to spy were cut out of the loop. Le Caron was advised not to send his reports in letters he addressed himself. Instead, his wife, Nannie, began sending the reports in letters addressed to a female relative of Robert Anderson, Home Office adviser on political crime.

Nannie had demonstrated both coolness and courage when she rescued her future husband and his comrades from marauding rebels on Christmas Eve 1862. Her bravery continued throughout their married life. Although she repeatedly begged her husband to stop working as a double agent, she was unwavering in her loyalty and support. Le Caron later paid tribute to her "courageous heart" in his autobiography:

> *A look, a gasp, a frightened movement, an uncertain turn might have betrayed me, ... a jealous action, a curious impulse, and she might have wrecked my life; a letter misplaced, a drawer left open, a communication miscarried, and my end was certain. But those things were not to be. Brave, affectionate, and fearless ... she ... faced the world with a countenance which gave no sign, but a caution which never slumbered.*

There was good reason for caution, as there was no predicting where or when danger would appear. In November 1868, John O'Neill asked Le Caron to visit Montreal and make contact with Fenian supporters there. Knowing that the Canadian government was eager to find out what it could about Fenians in Montreal, Toronto, and Kingston, Le Caron agreed.

To prepare for the trip, he spoke to John Roche, a prominent New York Fenian who had once lived in Montreal. Roche gladly provided several names but was greatly disturbed when he saw Le Caron jot the information down in a notebook instead of committing it to memory. A few weeks later, at the Fenians' annual convention in Philadelphia, he formally charged Le Caron with "carelessness, dangerous conduct and suspicious acts." An inquiry was then called. Le Caron had many friends in the organization, plus the support of John O'Neill, but decided the best strategy was to tender his resignation. It was refused and the charges were dropped. From that day forward, Le Caron never kept a notebook.

Over the next several months, Le Caron helped the Fenians prepare for another attack on Canada, all the while providing information to the British and Canadian governments. British authorities had put him in contact with Judge Gilbert McMicken, chief commissioner of the Dominion police. The spy network McMicken headed had originally been established to stop Confederate agents and sympathizers from using Canada as a base from which to strike at Union targets. Following the U.S. Civil War, McMicken's focus shifted to the Fenians.

Although McMicken had Canadian government agents in many locations along the U.S.–Canada border, Le Caron proved instrumental in filling some significant intelligence gaps. Soon after he had joined the Fenians, the Canadian government became convinced that another raid was imminent. However, Le Caron's reports made it clear that there was insufficient money to finance another attack, at least for a while.

But O'Neill was determined. Under his direction, Henri Le Caron inspected Fenian companies along the border and distributed 15,000 weapons and nearly 3 million rounds of ammunition. As he travelled through the northeastern states, he was often shadowed by a Canadian agent, John C. Rose, through whom he remained in contact with the Canadian government. Neither of them aroused suspicion until one day a visitor from Ottawa revealed Rose's occupation to the head of the Malone, New York, branch of Fenians. After tailing Rose for a while, the Fenians concluded he was a spy. He was robbed and severely beaten. Le Caron lost a valuable colleague and, ironically, had to praise his assailants for a job well done.

By the spring of 1870, it was clear that the Fenians were once again poised to invade Canada. In late May, a force assembled at Franklin, Vermont, close to the Quebec border. More men were expected but did not arrive on schedule. On May 25, O'Neill and about 200 men crossed the border into Canada. At Eccles Hill, Canadian militia opened fire, killing one Fenian and wounding two others. Disheartened, they began to retreat, but O'Neill used his force of character and rhetorical skill to rally them. They again faced the Canadians and returned fire.

According to Le Caron, there was brief lull as a Fenian contingent from St. Albans, Vermont, approached. As he supervised arrangements for their participation in the battle, he heard someone shout, "Clear the road! Clear the road!" A "furiously driven team of horses" raced by, pulling a covered carriage. Inside Le Caron saw "the dejected face of O'Neill, who was seated between two men." A U.S. Marshal had been waiting for the Fenian leader and arrested him for violating neutrality laws.

"To have given the command to shoot the horses as they turned an adjacent corner would have been the work of an instant," Le Caron later wrote, "but it was no part of my purpose to restore O'Neill to his command."

The next day, General Spear, the Fenians' secretary of war, reached St. Albans and tried to salvage the situation. He asked Le Caron to supply between 400 and 500 guns, plus ammunition, within 24 hours. Le Caron insisted this would be impossible. In the wake of the raid, thousands of Canadian troops had reached the border, severely hampering the Fenians' movements.

On Friday, April 27, Le Caron left the Fenian troops with the excuse that he was going to Burlington, Vermont, to see John O'Neill. Instead, he went to Rouses Point, New York, then to Montreal, where he reported to Judge Charles Coursel, one of McMicken's colleagues. On Saturday, he took the morning train for Ottawa. As usual, the train stopped at Cornwall and passengers took advantage of the half-hour delay to eat lunch.

Le Caron was enjoying his meal when a commotion broke out in the dining room. Looking around, he saw two men coming towards him — one of them a clergyman, the other a tall man with a distinct military bearing. As they approached, the preacher pointed at Le Caron and said to his companion, "That is the man." The taller man, who happened to be the mayor of Cornwall, moved forward, grasped Le Caron by the shoulder and, in a thick Scottish accent, announced, "You are my prisoner."

Le Caron subsequently learned the clergyman was a travelling preacher. Some time earlier, when Le Caron was planting weapons in Malone, New York, someone had pointed him out to the preacher as a Fenian agent. When he saw Le Caron in the station dining room, he immediately alerted authorities.

Despite the fact that he must have been sick with apprehension, he remained cool. He even had the nerve to ask his captors to let him finish dinner. The mayor refused. He was unceremoniously hustled to a room next to the ticket office, where he was told to hand over his luggage, his keys, and everything else in his possession. "My position was dangerous — distinctly dangerous," Le Caron recalled, for in his one piece of hand luggage were a number of documents relating to Fenian activities.

Le Caron asked for a few moments alone with the mayor and as quickly as possible explained the situation. Yes, he was posing as a Fenian, but he was really a government agent. "To delay or expose me would mean serious difficulty for the Government," Le Caron explained. Then he suggested a plan of action: send him under guard to Judge McMicken in

Ottawa, where matters could be sorted out. In the meantime, the mayor should also send a telegram advising McMicken of his imminent arrival. The mayor complied, assigning Le Caron a lieutenant who had just returned from the fighting with a Canadian regiment, along with a couple of other guards.

Le Caron's journey to the nation's capital was far from comfortable. In no time, most of the passengers learned that he was a Fenian and several crowded into the carriage, hissing, hooting, and shouting, "Hang him!" Fortunately, he made it without incident to Ottawa, where he and his captors were met by a representative from McMicken and taken to the police commissioner.

Convinced he was safe, Le Caron laughed with relief when brought before the judge, but McMicken greeted him solemnly. He asked the lieutenant for the details of the capture, formally took Le Caron into custody, and issued a receipt acknowledging the transfer. Only when the escort was safely on its way back to Cornwall did McMicken relax and greet Le Caron cordially. The secret agent stayed with the judge until nightfall then was transported to a local gentlemen's club.

McMicken told several of the more discreet members of the club the true identity of his guest, and within a short time Le Caron found himself welcomed as "the hero of the hour." After a pleasant evening and an overnight stay at the club, he was sent on his way.

Throughout these hectic years, Le Caron kept up his medical practice, which prospered thanks to his Fenian connections. Eventually, he also owned three drug stores. To his patients and friends, he was a successful doctor — the epitome of the American dream.

Le Caron continued to supply both the Canadian and British governments with information about Fenian activities. No doubt he was pleased when, after an 1871 raid in Manitoba, the Fenians never again posed a serious threat to Canada. However, they were still a threat to Britain, so Le Caron kept up his espionage work.

In the 1880s, he uncovered information about a Fenian plot against England involving dynamite attacks. While not able to stop all of the attacks, Le Caron did provide intelligence that resulted in the arrest of 25 terrorists. In 1881, he also came into contact with Charles Stewart Parnell, the Irish political leader who was suspected of Fenian connections.

For the next several years, Le Caron amassed considerable evidence that suggested Parnell was deeply involved in plots to overthrow the British government. Finally, in 1889, after nearly a quarter of a century as a spy, Le Caron decided to risk his safety by testifying against Parnell when the Irish nationalist was accused of being linked to various crimes, including murder. In doing so, he knew he was ending his career as a spy. He was also cutting ties with the United States, for to return would endanger his own life, and possibly that of his family.

The trial was highly publicized, and Le Caron's double life was thrown open to public scrutiny. Some criticized Le Caron for taking money for his espionage work, but Le Caron silenced most of them with his obvious patriotism. Many who saw him testify were impressed with his prodigious memory, his coolness, and his poise. Ultimately, Parnell was vindicated, but his political career collapsed soon afterwards.

During and after the trial, Le Caron and his family lived under police protection in London, England, where he assumed the name Dr. Howard. In 1892, he published his autobiography, *Twenty-five Years in the Secret Service: the Recollections of a Spy.*

After years of exile, Le Caron was apparently looking forward to a pleasant retirement in the land of his birth, surrounded by his nearest and dearest. Then, in the spring of 1894, he developed appendicitis. Since doctors of the time refused to operate if the patient was running a fever, nothing was done and peritonitis set in. He died on April 1, 1894, and was buried in Norwood Cemetery.

The cross marking his final resting place was inscribed with nothing more than a name, Henri Le Caron. As a result of the Parnell trial and Le Caron's memoir, the world knew his true identity was Thomas Billis Beach. But even in death, the master spy preferred to keep his true identity obscured.

Chapter 6
The Celebrated Chief: Long Lance

In the summer of 1924, English writer Eldred Walker toured Canada. While staying at the Banff Springs Hotel, an exclusive establishment in the Rocky Mountains, he wandered out onto the veranda and encountered an elegantly dressed man in his mid-30s. Walker soon discovered the charming young man was the assistant press representative for the hotel. Over drinks, the pair had a long conversation about various topics, including sports, agriculture, and the arts. After a while, Walker found himself staring at his companion's bronze skin, high cheekbones, dark brown eyes, and slick black hair. Sensing the reason for his curiosity, the younger man asked the portly British writer, "Can you tell to what nationality I belong?" When Walker could not, his companion introduced himself as Chief Buffalo Child Long Lance, a "full-blooded Indian."

Recounting the conversation in his book *Canadian Trails Revisited*, Walker wrote, "Had the heavens opened, I could not have had a greater surprise."

Walker might have been even more surprised to learn

Chief Buffalo Child Long Lance, 1890-1932

that Long Lance's revelation was a lie. But then, Sylvester Long would have been equally astounded if Walker had not believed him. The young man had spent much of his life spinning lies in order to escape the poverty and prejudice of his origins in the U.S. South.

He was born on December 1, 1890, in a black neighbourhood of Winston-Salem, North Carolina. His parents, Joe and Sallie Long, claimed their ancestry was Native and white, but in all likelihood they also had some black antecedents. Natives and blacks frequently intermarried in the U.S. South. Furthermore, Sallie Long identified with the Croatans — also known as Lumbees — whose mixed origins included Natives, black slaves, and the survivors of the lost English settlement of Roanoke, Virginia.

But Joe and Sallie had been slaves, which was enough to classify them as "coloured." In towns with significant Native communities, the Longs would have been identified with them and been accorded higher status than blacks, but that option did not exist in Winston-Salem. Joe, Sallie, and their children were considered black. In the segregated South, this meant they had limited opportunities. Blacks typically held the lowest-paying, most menial jobs, but Joe and Sallie Long were exceptionally fortunate. Sallie nursed both black and white families, while Joe was a clerk, and later a janitor in a white high school.

Sylvester grew up with little knowledge of his native heritage. He was, however, fully aware of the limitations imposed by the circumstances of his birth, and he chafed at them. He was bright, imaginative, and ambitious, and did not relish the thought of spending his life in a dead-end, subservient job. At age 13, after finishing Grade 6 at the Depot Street School for Negroes in 1903, he joined a circus.

With his coppery skin and straight black hair, he easily passed for a Native. Since he had always been fascinated with the Wild West, this suited him perfectly. But the job ended after a few months and he returned to Winston-Salem, where he went to work as a janitor at the new public library. The work was boring, but he had easy access to the library's books, and he read voraciously.

By 1908, he had saved enough to attend a private school. But Sylvester was 18, much older than the other students, and probably felt embarrassed to be in the same classes. By October, he was on the road again, this time with Robinson's Circus. Always athletic, he became an expert horseman. He also became friendly with Allen Whipporwill, an Eastern Cherokee who taught him some basics of the Cherokee language.

Back home again in the summer of 1909, he decided to teach himself typing, a skill that might lead to better employment opportunities. Unable to afford a typewriter, he borrowed the keys to the white high school where his father was janitor and let himself into the office after hours. One day, the principal came in unexpectedly and caught him hammering at the typewriter. Technically, Sylvester was trespassing, as well as using school equipment without permission, and the principal could have had him arrested. But the Longs were well-respected in the community and the principal was impressed with Sylvester's initiative. He sent for Joe and suggested that, if Sylvester so desperately wanted an education, something should be done. Knowing the Longs' Native connections, he suggested Sylvester apply to the Carlisle Indian Residential School in Carlisle, Pennsylvania.

Renowned across the United States, the school ran along military lines and trained Native students from all across the country for jobs in trades or domestic service. Sylvester had the academic qualifications required, but there were two major obstacles. First of all, students at Carlisle had to be between 14 and 18 years old. Sylvester was nearly 19, but decided to lie about his age, shifting his birth date from 1890 to 1891. Secondly, he had to provide proof of Native ancestry. Sallie Long was only one-quarter Native. Joe Long claimed Cherokee ancestry, but he was not listed on the tribal rolls. Nevertheless, to ensure that Sylvester had the best possible chance, Joe Long listed himself as half Cherokee and his wife as half Croatan. Joe then had two prominent citizens, one black and one white, sign statements confirming that Sylvester was regarded as "Indian" within the community.

The deception worked. Sylvester was accepted at Carlisle. There, even though there were several students who suspected he had black ancestry, he won many friends. He worked hard, excelling in many areas including sports and debating. Of medium height but very muscular, he played football and also made the track team, where one of the other members was future Olympic medallist Jim Thorpe. The pair trained together and Thorpe later credited their practices with helping him win the pentathlon and decathlon at the 1912 Stockholm Olympics.

After graduating from Carlisle, Sylvester enrolled in St. John's Military Academy, in upstate New York. Again he changed his birth date — this time back to 1890 — but he also moved his place of birth farther east to reinforce his claim of Cherokee blood. In addition, he no longer called himself Sylvester Long, but Sylvester Chahuska Long Lance. During his years at Carlisle, he had absorbed much Native culture and he used the knowledge to reinforce his identity as a Cherokee.

Long Lance did very well at St. John's, both as an athlete and a scholar. He began to consider a military career. Inspired by the confidence he had developed since leaving North Carolina, he took aim at West Point, the most prestigious military school in the United States. As a Cherokee, his chances of acceptance were slim, but Long Lance was as daring as he was ambitious. He wrote directly to President Woodrow Wilson, asking for an appointment to West Point.

His boldness paid off, bolstered by glowing recommendations from staff members at Carlisle and St. John's. In May 1915, the U.S. War Department informed him that he could attend West Point, providing he passed the entrance exams the following spring. Newspapers across the country picked up the story, eager for some good news in the aftermath of the sinking of the *Lusitania* by a German U-boat. Some of the papers, including the *Twin City Daily Sentinel* in Winston-Salem, carried a photograph as well as the story, which described Long Lance as "a full-blooded Cherokee."

Long Lance revelled in the attention. While still at Carlisle, he had achieved some public recognition by writing for school publications. He had also got his name in the newspapers a few years earlier when he helped search for a lost child. Every time he was mentioned in print, he clipped the story and pasted it in a scrapbook. Publicity became very important to him, almost as if he needed it to prove his success and confirm his identity. For the rest of his life, Long Lance would go out of his way to attract attention. Yet, even as early as 1915, he realized that celebrity had a price.

Having reinvented himself as a Cherokee, he could no longer return home, where he and his family were still viewed as "coloured." And perhaps, for a little while, he may have considered that the cost of keeping up his masquerade was too high.

In March 1916, he went to Fort Slocum, near New Rochelle, New York, for the entrance examinations to West Point. He passed the physical easily then began the three-day ordeal of writing six tests. He failed three, even though he had passed the same subjects with flying colours at St. John's. Possibly he had succumbed to nerves, but biographer Donald

B. Smith suggests otherwise — namely that Long Lance had heard that the War Department had made inquiries into his background, and he may have decided the risk of discovery was too great. In any event, when he later described his failure in his highly fictionalized autobiography, he claimed it was deliberate. Rather than spending years at West Point, he wrote, he wanted to get to the front lines and join the forces fighting in Europe. As soon as the tests were done, he headed for Canada to join the army.

In fact, he did not enlist until August 1916. Sent to France, he proved himself a good soldier, if not an outstanding one. He fought at Vimy and emerged unscathed, but was hit in the head with shrapnel and had his nose broken a month later. After a couple of weeks' convalescence, he returned to the front and was again injured, this time seriously enough to be out of the fighting for the duration.

After the war, he returned to Canada and headed for Calgary, Alberta. He knew no one, had no job prospects, and still had to overcome the prejudice against Natives that prevailed in the Canadian West. It took a few weeks, but his dashing appearance, the persuasiveness of his manner, and an impressive application finally convinced Charles Hayden, managing editor of the *Calgary Herald*, to hire him as a reporter.

Once more, however, Long Lance had twisted the truth, exaggerating facts or making them up in order to get what he wanted. Although he had never risen higher than acting sergeant, he claimed he had been a captain during the war. He also said he had received the Cross de Guerre, that he had fought in Italy, and that he had attended West Point. There was not a drop of truth in any of those claims. Nor was there any truth in the story he circulated about his origins. Wishing to be more closely identified with the Native peoples of the western plains, he changed his birthplace to Oklahoma, where many Cherokees had been forcibly relocated in 1838.

Again, Sylvester Long Lance was fortunate. Although it would have been a relatively easy matter to check his war record, if nothing else, no one bothered. Instead, they accepted him at face value. And, since he was charming, outgoing, athletic, and hard-working, just about everyone he met was willing to accept what he told them. He was popular with his co-workers and many others he met in Calgary. He was also popular with the ladies, dating many white women at a time when interracial dating was very controversial.

One of his friends, reporter Ralph Wilson, described him as "a dashing, handsome Indian who always ended up with the most beautiful girl." And yet there was no question of marrying one of those beautiful girls, as Long Lance realized. Mixed marriages did occur, but were generally frowned upon by society. In addition, Long Lance may have worried about the consequences of having children. Although he and his parents insisted there was no black blood in the family, Long Lance apparently had his suspicions. If he fathered a child with Negroid features, his masquerade would be revealed. Long Lance did not want to take that risk.

Instead, he remained a bachelor and concentrated on his career. He could write almost anything and excelled at sports stories, but it was his series on the Native peoples of Alberta that set him on the road to international fame. Because he presented himself as a "full-blooded Indian," and because he was so urbane and eloquent, he attracted plenty of attention. His articles, which also appeared in the *Vancouver Sun* and *Winnipeg Tribune*, were republished in national magazines, including *Maclean's*.

Eventually his work led to speaking engagements. One of his favourite topics was "The Red Man, Past and Present." In print or in person, Long Lance was always entertaining, even if he was not always accurate. Throughout his career, he had no compunction about changing facts in order to tell a good story, a practice that he had been applying to his own life for almost two decades.

When he had first arrived on the Canadian prairies in 1918, he presented himself as a Cherokee. By August 1927, in a series for the *Vancouver Sun*, he was referring to his "fellow-tribesmen, the Blood Indians of Alberta." There was, in fact, a grain of truth to the claim. In February 1922, St. Paul's mission school on the Blood reserve near Macleod, Alberta, held a student reunion. Long Lance, who had made many friends there, was formally adopted into the tribe during the reunion and given the name Buffalo Child. He was not the first individual, Native or white, to be so honoured.

But "Chief Buffalo Child Long Lance," as he styled himself, exploited the privilege for his own purposes.

The man who had once been plain Sylvester Long had become addicted to celebrity. Because a large part of his fame was based on his Native persona, he reminded the public of it as often as possible.

Yet, even though he had interviewed many Native people for his newspaper and magazine articles, he frequently made mistakes that underscored the distance between his own sensibilities and those of people who had grown up within Native cultures. One notorious example occurred in Regina in 1923, when he had two photographs taken in "tribal regalia." To the unschooled eye, he looked like a genuine "Indian," but in fact he was wearing a Blackfoot vest, a Blood pouch, Crow pants (which he managed to put on backwards), and a long, braided wig.

That summer, he visited the Blackfoot reserve to gather information about the Sun Dance, one of the tribe's most sacred ceremonies. In the past when he visited reserves, he had usually been accompanied by an interpreter, missionary, or Indian agent, who made introductions and helped ease any tension. This time, he was largely on his own, and he quickly revealed his ignorance about Native culture. He was too inquisitive, too eager to publicize the details of sacred ceremonies, oblivious to etiquette that should have been second nature to someone who claimed kinship with the people of the plains. Ultimately, he upset many of the tribal elders, who felt he behaved more like a white man than a Native. But this did not stop him from writing extensively about the Sun Dance ceremony, even though he had to make up many of the details.

One of the reasons he managed to get away with his outrageous claims and fictionalized articles was that relatively few people in positions of power actually knew any Natives. Most assumed that the suave, eloquent, educated "Chief" was a shining example of the effect of "civilization" on the "red man." Long Lance used that perception to full advantage, not only while employed at the Banff Springs Hotel, but also when work took him to New York City to cover various sports events. In no time at all he was hobnobbing with the rich and famous, including wealthy businessmen and entertainers. Eventually, those connections led to a series of articles for *Cosmopolitan* magazine, which in turn led to a book contract.

Ray Long, who was editor-in-chief of *Cosmopolitan*, was also involved in the Cosmopolitan Book Corporation. In March 1927, he sat down with Long Lance to discuss a book. Initially, it was supposed to be a kind of adventure story for boys, but it gradually morphed into a first-person story. Published the following year, it opened with dramatic action:

> *The first thing in my life that I can remember*
> *is the exciting aftermath of an Indian fight*
> *in northern Montana. My mother was crying*

and running about with me in my moss bag-carrier on her back. I remember the scene as thought it were yesterday, yet I was barely a year old. Women and horses were everywhere, but I remember only two women: my mother and my aunt.

Long Lance: The Autobiography of a Blackfoot Chief was an instant best seller. Although much of it was fiction, the book was praised by academics as well as the general public, went into a second printing, and was translated into German and Dutch. With the book selling briskly in North America, Britain, and Europe, Long Lance was probably the most famous Native North American of the era. Partly as a result of the book's success, he was asked to star in a movie, *The Silent Enemy.*

Douglas Burden, a young naturalist and explorer, wanted to make a docudrama about Native North Americans. Although the storyline was fictitious and included a romance to appeal to cinema fans, Burden's idea was to create a movie that depicted pre-contact Ojibwa as accurately as possible. To achieve this, he selected northern Ontario and Quebec as the setting, and carefully chose a cast made up of "real" Indians. Long Lance starred as Baluk, the hunter responsible for saving his people from hunger, "the silent enemy."

True to character, Long Lance threw himself into the role with determination and élan. He impressed the crew with his good humour, his punctuality, and his professional-ism. Nearly every day, despite near-freezing temperatures, he swam outdoors then worked out for at least an hour. Always supremely fit and physically daring, he handled his own stunts. In one scene, he rescues Neewa, his sweetheart, from a charging she-bear. This was in the days before animals were protected on movie sets, and the bear was actually killed during filming. Although the fatal arrow was shot by some-one else, Long Lance personally collected the two orphaned cubs and presented them to Neewa — acquiring several deep scratches in the process. In another scene in which a moose was killed, he wielded the spear himself.

Impressive as Long Lance was, his involvement in *The Silent Enemy* led to problems. Chauncey Yellow Robe, a Sioux who played the Ojibwa chief in the movie, grew up on the plains in the 1870s and 1880s and attended Carlisle Indian Residential School. He soon suspected that Long Lance was not who he claimed to be. For one thing, the buffalo herds he had described in his autobiography had disappeared long before he had been born. In addition, Long Lance frequently made mistakes in sign language, although he often gave public demonstrations of his expertise. There were other hints, including a way of dancing that was completely unlike anything Yellow Robe had seen on the plains.

The Silent Enemy opened on May 19, 1930, at the Criterion Theatre in Times Square. It was critically acclaimed and Long Lance, as usual, received a great deal of praise for his work. But in the months immediately preceding the premiere, Long Lance's intricately created world had begun to fall apart.

Ironically, the problems started with the fictionalized autobiography. Shortly before the book was printed, Ray Long sent a complimentary advance copy to Charles Burke, at the U.S. Office of Indian Affairs. Long was probably hoping to get a quotable response that could be used to promote the book. Instead, Burke took it upon himself to find out more about the author. He wrote to several people, including the U.S. War Department, about Long Lance's West Point connection, and also corresponded with Percy Little Dog, an acquaintance who happened to be the interpreter for the Blood council in Alberta.

In response to his inquiries, he learned that Sylvester Long Lance had failed the West Point examination and that he was more likely a Cherokee than a Blood or Blackfoot. "He ... has no tribal rights on the Reserve," Percy Little Dog informed him. "We have heard he was a Cherokee Indian, but we do not know definitely who he is and where he came from." Diplomatically, Charles Burke responded to Ray Long by acknowledging the receipt of "a publication of fiction" although he admitted it was "very interesting and quite readable."

Worse was to come. Before *The Silent Enemy* was released, Douglas Burden and his partner, lawyer William Chanler, heard rumours that Long Lance was not who he claimed to be. Chanler investigated and confronted Long Lance with the accusation that he was not a full-blooded chief from the plains but a Croatan — a person of mixed Native and Black blood. Long Lance denied everything, then concocted yet another story about his origins. Thoroughly confused, Chanler investigated further, sending Ilia Tolstoy to North Carolina to investigate. Tolstoy, who had been assistant director for *The Silent Enemy*, was the grandson of the famous Russian novelist and something of an adventurer in his own right. He liked Long Lance and considered him a friend. In Winston-Salem, he talked to members of the Long family and reported that, while Long Lance may not have been a Blood, he was at least part Cherokee.

Meanwhile, Long Lance had confided the details of his early life to Chauncey Yellow Robe, his co-star in *The Silent Enemy*. Understanding the courage and tenacity it took to rise above the racial prejudices of his birthplace, Yellow Robe expressed admiration for the younger man. When he fell ill in March 1930, just as the publicity campaign for *The Silent Enemy* was getting underway, Yellow Robe asked that Long Lance take his place.

He was a natural as a promoter, once more revelling in the attention and thrilling audiences with his handsome appearance and impressive presence. But the persistent rumours that he was at least part black turned many former friends against him.

Life began to sour for Long Lance as he approached

forty. Apart from his personal troubles, the stock market had crashed in October 1929, putting a serious damper on the New York social scene that he loved.

Although still as charming as ever, he was drinking more heavily. Still, he seemed to land on his feet once more when he found a wealthy patron, Anita Baldwin. She hired him to accompany her as secretary and bodyguard on a trip to Europe in the fall of 1931. However, the trip did not go well. Later, she would recall that he was depressed and had attempted suicide more than once. Also, during one drunken episode, he had threatened to kill a companion. When Anita and her party returned from Europe, she left Long Lance in New York instead of taking him back to her estate in California as originally planned.

While in New York, he fell in love with Bessie Clapp, a young white dancer from Greenwich Village. Although she was willing to marry him, he was still afraid of a mixed-race union so he ended the affair. Then, after contacting Anita, he fled west to Anoakia, her sumptuous estate in southern California.

He arrived in late December. Anita, who was considerably older than Long Lance, forgave him for his previous bad behaviour and welcomed him. There was talk of an expedition to South America to explore some Mayan ruins, and Anita also renewed a promise to buy an airplane for Long Lance, who had recently taken up flying.

But friction developed between them in a very short

time. Long Lance was frequently at loose ends, with little to occupy his time but reading, flying, and socializing. He drank too much and frequently tormented the men who guarded the estate — so much so that they threatened to shoot him. He deliberately provoked Anita by telling her about his many romantic liaisons in New York. After a few weeks, Long Lance left the estate and booked into the Glendale Hotel.

Meanwhile Anita, who was as paranoid as she was wealthy, began to worry about her safety and that of her family, especially after the young son of aviator Charles Lindbergh was kidnapped and murdered. A woman of strong and often irrational opinions, she was convinced that gangsters were taking over the country and that vigilante justice was acceptable to keep them under control. She strongly disapproved of Long Lance's heavy drinking, as well as the new friends he had made in California. For reasons that are not quite clear, but may have included suspicions about black ancestry, Anita hired a detective to follow Long Lance.

Around March 18, Bessie Clapp — the dancer Long Lance had fallen for in New York — called Long Lance to announce that she had married a Japanese man. On the night of March 19, 1932, after dinner and a movie, he took a taxi to Anita's estate. According to the clerk at his hotel, he had been drinking and was carrying his gun, a .45 revolver for which he had a permit. When he reached Anoakia, Anita answered the door herself. According to her version of the events, they had gone to the library to talk but he was "quite abrupt, very depressed and non-communicative." Not wanting to spend time in his company while he was in a bad mood, Anita returned to her room. A short time later, she heard a shot. She roused one of her watchmen, who rushed to the library. Long Lance was sprawled on a settee, his legs stretched out, a gun in his hand, and a bullet in his head.

Friends and acquaintances were shocked to learn of the suicide, and many could not believe it was true. Among them was humorist Irvin S. Cobb, who had written the foreword to Sylvester's biography. When he learned about rumours that Long Lance was black, he was furious that he had offered him the hospitality of his home. "We're so ashamed! We entertained a nigger," he raged, displaying the kind of racism that had inspired Long Lance's masquerade. But, when Cobb heard of Long Lance's death, he said he could not believe that "so gallant a man as he was ever deliberately took his own life." Cobb was not alone in his assessment.

In Cobb's opinion, the police investigation was a farce. In fact, without the insistence of two prominent Native women, there would not have been any inquiry at all. As it was, the proceedings were both hasty and superficial. The inquiry was held in Arcadia, close to Anoakia. Anita Baldwin had enormous influence in the community, where she paid half the property taxes. Because of this, she was not required to appear for questioning, but merely submitted a written statement. In addition, several of the witnesses were on Anita's payroll.

Some of Anita's evidence described Long Lance's depression and suicide attempts during the trip to Europe. While there was little doubt that he had been drinking heavily at the time, there were those who wondered whether the "evidence" of suicidal tendencies had been concocted to cover up a murder.

J. H. Williams, the night clerk at the Glendale Hotel, told one of Long Lance's friends that there was much more to the story but he could not reveal the details without damaging the hotel's reputation.

The result of the inquest was a foregone conclusion — death by suicide. Certainly it was a possibility. Heavy drinking, Bessie's marriage, and his increasingly precarious financial situation would have taken a serious toll on Long Lance's emotional health. Added to these were the years of pretending and the constant fear of discovery. As Chief Buffalo Child Long Lance, Sylvester Long had proved he was a consummate actor, perfectly capable of deceiving those who thought they knew him best. He might also have been capable of hiding his fears, desperation, and loneliness from them.

A thorough, well-documented inquiry might have revealed more about his character and motivation than anything he had written or said during his lifetime, and most definitely it should have revealed the truth about his final hours. In the end, however, the circumstances of his death were as confusing as those of his life.

Chapter 7
The Conservationist: Grey Owl

O xford City Hall was packed. Hundreds of people, many of them university students, had turned out on a late January evening in 1936 to hear the "modern Hiawatha" deliver his message. The audience grew silent as a tall, handsome Native man appeared. Dressed in intricately beaded buckskin, his dark hair parted and adorned with a single eagle feather, Grey Owl raised his hand and greeted the audience with two words, "How Kola," which means "hello, friend" in Sioux. They were immediately mesmerized.

For several weeks, the Canadian writer and conservationist had been speaking to British audiences about the need to preserve the wilderness and the animals it harboured, especially his beloved beavers. He also urged better treatment of Native peoples. In simple, eloquent language, he presented his case, illustrating his points with films of the tame beavers that were his companions in Saskatchewan's

Grey Owl, 1888-1938

Prince Albert National Park. By the end of the tour, tens of thousands had heard him and many had purchased copies of his books.

Members of the Oxford audience who had already read his works were familiar with Grey Owl's account of his early life. His father was a Scot who had lived in Texas and married an Apache woman. Grey Owl himself had been born in Mexico. After his father was killed in a shoot-out, he was raised by his mother's people in the Southwest. At the age of 10, Grey Owl knew fewer than 100 words of English. Then he travelled extensively with Buffalo Bill's Wild West show before settling in northern Ontario, then northern Quebec.

Like many men of Native ancestry, Grey Owl lived close to the land. He was an expert canoeist. He hunted for food and to earn money, trapping beavers and other fur-bearing animals for several seasons. And then he met Gertrude Bernard and his life took a surprising turn.

In the summer of 1925, they were both working at Camp Wabikon on Lake Temagami. She was a 19-year-old waitress of Mohawk ancestry who was planning to finish her education in the fall. He was a 36-year-old guide with no real prospects. But the attraction between them was mutual. As Gertie would later write, Archie, as he was known, was "tall, straight, and handsome .... What really set my imagination afire was his long hair and wide-brimmed hat .... In my imagination, this man looked like the ever so thrilling hero of my youth, Jesse James."

Nevertheless, she went home to Mattawa. For weeks, Archie wrote to her and eventually persuaded her to join him for the winter. Gertie agreed, although she had never been involved in trapping before. Nor did she have much experience at paddling a canoe. Archie taught her all he could and even gave her a new name, Anahareo, a variation on the name of one of her ancestors.

After several months together, Archie and Anahareo were married in a native ceremony. They continued to live off the land, but Anahareo was becoming increasingly uncomfortable with the horrible suffering of animals caught in traps.

In the spring of 1928, Archie trapped two adult beavers. It was late in the season, and he realized that the pair's kittens would not be able to survive on their own. Rather than have them suffer, he decided to trap them. But when he and Anahareo spotted the young beavers, Anahareo could not bear the thought of killing them. Instead, she persuaded Archie to adopt the kittens.

For most of the next year, Archie and Anahareo raised the two young beavers, which they named McGinnis and McGinty. They were amazed at the animals' intelligence, their curiosity, and their affection. Other people also became intrigued when they encountered the tame beavers. Meanwhile, Archie had begun to write of his wilderness experiences for British and Canadian magazines.

Then McGinnis and McGinty suddenly vanished, possibly killed by a hunter or trapper. Archie and Anahareo were inconsolable, for the young beavers had already left an indelible mark on their lives. Archie, who knew first-hand that Canada's national animal was quickly disappearing, decided to start a crusade to save them. He had read about the successful reintroduction of the buffalo in the West and was convinced that he could do the same for the beaver by establishing a protected colony for them.

One of his first steps was to tame another young beaver. Jelly Roll was just as intelligent and adaptable as the Macs had been and nearly as affectionate. In the summer of 1929, hoping to raise money for the beaver colony, Archie and Anahareo took Jelly Roll to Métis-sur-Mer, a resort for English-speaking Montrealers located near Rivière-du-Loup, Quebec. A hastily organized lecture brought impressive results. Not only did Archie and Anahareo raise $700 for their cause, they also met some influential people, including Colonel Wilfrid Bovey, an administrator at McGill University. The audience was amazed by the mesmerizing voice and intriguing message of the long-haired "half-breed" who spoke as eloquently as any highly educated white man.

Anahareo and his long-time acquaintances still called him Archie. But Grey Owl was how the public knew him, and that public was rapidly growing. In November 1929, Jean-Charles Harvey of the Quebec City newspaper *Le Soleil* interviewed him. He was deeply impressed with what Grey Owl was trying to do. But Harvey also noted the increasing tension between Grey Owl and Anahareo. At the time, Grey Owl was writing his first book and was so absorbed in the task that he neglected his wife. Fiercely independent, Anahareo decided she would pursue her own dreams and left for a winter of prospecting in northern Ontario.

The following year, Grey Owl was a guest speaker at

the Canadian Forestry Association's annual convention in Montreal. He was an immediate hit, not only because of his great speaking ability but because of a film commissioned by the Canadian Park Branch commissioner James Harkin. The silent movie showed Jelly Roll and a tame male beaver, Rawhide, interacting with Grey Owl.

As a result of his speaking engagement, Grey Owl was interviewed by the *Montreal Star*, one of Canada's most prestigious newspapers. His fame spread rapidly after that, especially after *Men of the Last Frontier* was published in 1931. That same year, recognizing his value as a tourist attraction, government officials invited Grey Owl to live in Riding Mountain National Park, Manitoba, as a caretaker. As part of the deal, he brought Jelly Roll and Rawhide along. A short time later he transferred to a specially designed lodge on Lake Ajawaan in Prince Albert National Park. Beaver Lodge, as it was named, was custom-built to allow Jelly Roll and Rawhide to enter at will.

As the resident celebrity, Grey Owl had many visitors, including Governor General Lord Tweedsmuir and future prime minister John Diefenbaker. He could be charming and hospitable, especially if the visitors seemed genuinely interested in nature, conservation, and the beavers. But he could also be surly and silent if he chose.

Grey Owl was not an easy character to deal with. He drank excessively and could become extremely belligerent. When he was writing, he ignored just about everyone around him, including Anahareo, who returned to live with him periodically and bore a daughter, Dawn, in August 1932. She finally left him for good, although she continued to be an influential presence in both his films and books.

Those books made Grey Owl famous. In 1934, he published *Pilgrims of the Wild,* followed in 1935 by a children's book, *The Adventures of Sajo and Her Beaver People.* That year, a second film was shot, this time at Prince Albert National Park. And, at the instigation of his new British publisher, Lovat Dickson, he gave a highly successful lecture tour in Britain in 1935. For several weeks he spoke nearly every day, sometimes three times a day, to crowds as large as 3,000 people.

He fascinated British audiences on a number of levels. First, there was the striking contrast between his Native appearance — his beaded buckskin costume, long hair, and stoic manner — and his outstanding command of the English language. Secondly, and perhaps more importantly, was his message that the wilderness must be preserved. Most of Britain's wilderness had vanished long before 1935, and the idea that there was somewhere on earth where wild animals and "primitive" peoples still roamed freely appealed to both nature-lovers and romantics.

Grey Owl was introduced to many people during his tour, and in some cases welcomed into their homes. One such home belonged to "two maiden ladies" who, he told friends, had provided him a place to stay while he was recuperating from a serious wound during the First World War.

In 1937, after the publication of another book, *Tales of an Empty Cabin,* Grey Owl returned to Britain. This time he was accompanied by a new wife, Yvonne, and also had another film to show audiences. Once again he visited the "two maiden ladies" in Hastings. He also gave a command performance for King George VI, Queen Elizabeth, the Princesses Elizabeth and Margaret, and Mary, the queen mother. Again, he kept up an incessant pace, lecturing as many as three times a day, seldom stopping. Then it was back to North America for further touring in the United States and Canada.

Yvonne collapsed from exhaustion and was hospitalized, so Grey Owl returned alone to Beaver Lodge on April 4, 1938. He was ready to take up his seasonal duties, but the tour and his heavy drinking had taken their toll. By April 8, he was in hospital in Prince Albert. At first, he seemed to be resting comfortably. Then he developed a fever and slipped into a coma. On April 13, at 8:15 in the morning, the man many regarded as "the modern Hiawatha" died. He was not quite 50.

When news of his death reached the *North Bay Nugget,* city editor Ed Bunyan ran a story he had been sitting on since 1935. That year, 18-year-old Britt Jessup had followed up on a tip from Jim Graham, the owner of a Temagami restaurant. According to Graham, a local Ojibway woman had seen a newspaper photograph of Grey Owl and claimed he was her husband. Angle Belaney told a convincing story, which Jessup wrote up, but Bunyan decided not to publish it. With storm clouds gathering over Europe and the Great Depression still on, Canadians needed good news, not bad. Besides, Bunyan reasoned, Grey Owl's crusade to save the wilderness and improve conditions for Native peoples was more important than domestic problems and a bit of role-playing. Still, Grey Owl's questionable past was now something of an open secret among certain reporters.

In March 1937, Grey Owl had stopped in North Bay on his way to Abitibi. Mort Fellman, a local reporter, arranged to interview him. As usual, Grey Owl wore his Indian regalia — moccasins and buckskin clothing. And, as usual, he delivered his message so convincingly that the 25-year-old reporter was a bit overwhelmed. But Fellman also knew about Jessup's story. When he asked Grey Owl about the connection between Archie Belaney of the Temagami district, and himself, Grey Owl abruptly ended their meeting.

Fellman relayed this information to Ed Bunyan, who once again chose not to pursue it. However, when he learned of Grey Owl's death, there was no longer any reason to protect the "modern Hiawatha." The story ran in the *North Bay Nugget* and was quickly picked up by big-city dailies in Canada and Britain. Those closest to Grey Owl angrily denied the story, including his publisher Lovat Dickson and his boss at Prince Albert National Park, Superintendent Major James Wood. Then, on April 19, a reporter in Hastings, England, called on the two maiden ladies whom Grey Owl had visited during his British tours.

During a brief interview, Ada Belaney was tricked into admitting that Grey Owl was actually her nephew, Archie Belaney. A bit more digging revealed some details of Archie's childhood and youth including his fascination with American and Canadian Natives and a postwar marriage to a Hastings girl, Ivy Holmes. When Ivy was located and interviewed, she provided a few more details, including the fact that Archie had lost a toe as the result of a war injury. Back in Canada, a spokesman from the Prince Albert funeral parlour confirmed that Grey Owl was missing the same toe.

While the controversy gathered steam, Grey Owl was buried on Friday, April 15. The funeral chapel in Prince Albert was packed with friends and admirers, Canadian army veterans, trappers, and prospectors. Anahareo, the woman most widely identified with Grey Owl, was absent, but her young daughter, Dawn, sat quietly throughout the funeral before asking for a rose to keep in memory of her father. Once the service was over, the cortège drove to Prince Albert National Park, where Grey Owl was laid to rest between two gigantic elms on the shores of Lake Ajawaan.

It would take some time before all the details of Grey Owl's life were revealed, but eventually they were made public. Archibald Stansfeld Belaney had been born in Hastings, England, on September 18, 1888. His father, George, was from a prosperous middle-class family but lost most of his money and drank heavily. His mother was too young to care for him properly, and so Archie was raised by his maiden aunts, Ada and Carrie. He received a good education, excelling in the subjects that interested him and displaying a definite talent for writing. But Archie was a lonely child, isolated from his peers because of his unusual family circumstances. As a result, he took comfort in observing nature. He also developed a fascination with the American West, especially the native tribes, and was forever playing "Red Indian." While that was not unusual for a boy of his time, Archie took it far beyond the level of normal amusement, learning to walk, talk, shoot, and throw a knife in what he felt was true Indian fashion.

He also had a wild side that manifested itself in outlandish pranks and occasional outbursts of temper. Once he tipped a large bust off its pedestal in an attempt to injure one of his aunts. As a teenager, he was fired from his job as a clerk in a lumberyard after tossing a bag of lighted firecrackers down his employer's chimney. Because of his refusal to settle into a respectable occupation, his aunts finally gave into his pleas and in 1906 sent him to Canada, where he was supposed to work in agriculture.

Instead, he spent a few months in Toronto, possibly working as a clerk in a large department store. Then he headed for northern Canada, determined to learn to survive on the land, just like the Natives he had read about. He found a mentor, Bill Guppy, who taught him how to trap, snowshoe, chop wood, and throw an axe. Bill, his brothers, and Archie wintered on Lake Temiskaming, then canoed to Temagami and Bear Island.

The Conservationist: Grey Owl

For some reason, Archie returned to England in late 1907. But the next year, he was back in the Temagami area, where he slid into the persona that would eventually become Grey Owl. When walking on the streets of the northern Ontario town, he wore moccasins and a broad-brimmed hat. His English accent faded away and he picked up a number of words in Ojibwa, especially after meeting a young Ojibway woman, Angle Negenegwune. Archie was warmly welcomed by Angle's family. By 1910, he was formally adopted by the Bear Island Ojibwa, and, on August 23 of that year, he married Angle in a Christian ceremony.

All his life, Archie Belaney had wanted to live like a Native. Now he had the skills that allowed him work as a trapper and a wilderness guide, as well as a Native wife. But there was still considerable prejudice against Native Canadians in 1910, and some of the white men who had been friendly towards Archie before his marriage now snubbed him. Worse, Archie was unprepared for the responsibilities of married life and fatherhood. His daughter Agnes was born in the spring of 1911; by 1912, he had left her and Angle to live near Biscotasing, north of Sudbury.

In a new area, with all the skills a Native trapper might possess and some fluency in Ojibway, it was easier for Archie to pass as someone with Native or at least partly Native ancestry. And, since he was a gifted storyteller, many people believed him when he told them the fictional story of his mixed white and Native ancestry. In addition, Archie frequently drank too much and got into brawls, behaviour that fit right in with stereotypical images of Native North Americans.

His wilderness escapades ended when a warrant was issued for his arrest. He joined the army in the summer of 1914, shortly before the First World War began. Eventually, he went overseas, where he was assigned duties as a sniper. Injured in a gas attack and then shot in the foot, he was sent to England to recuperate and found his way back to his aunts in Hastings.

There, he reconnected with Ivy Holmes, a childhood friend, and they married in February 1917 — even though Archie was still legally married to Angle. By summer, they were planning to return to northern Ontario, but the war was not yet over and war brides were required to remain in Britain. So Ivy had to stay behind, although Archie promised to send for her as soon as he was settled.

They never met again. Instead, Archie went back to Angle for a little while, then left once more. Over the next several years, he eked out a living as a trapper and a guide, all the while embellishing the story of his origins. He also took great pains to look the part, dyeing his brown hair black and staining his skin with henna. As Harry Wood, a Hudson's Bay Company employee observed, "Nothing made Archie Belaney prouder than to be termed a full-blooded Indian. ... If he was standing around the store and some newcomers pointed him out as a 'real Indian' he was pleased as Punch."

As a further embellishment, Archie sometimes staged a war dance, along with several friends. Concocted more from his fertile imagination than from observation — and usually fuelled by alcohol — it bore little resemblance to anything authentic; but it certainly got attention. Invariably, Archie decked himself out in full native costume and pounded out the rhythm on a drum made from a wooden cheese box covered with deerskin. Often, he sang an accompaniment that sounded "authentic" to most observers but was actually sheer nonsense.

Yet no one questioned Archie too closely about the discrepancies in his behaviour or the stories of his origins. Even Anahareo, who probably knew Archie better than any living person, accepted him as Native.

When they had first met in 1925, he was still calling himself Archie Belaney and was receiving a disability pension in that name. In spite of his elaborate masquerade, at some level, he still considered himself non-native. In May 1929, he wrote to *Country Life*, the British magazine that was publishing his articles, referring to Natives as "them." Six months later, in another letter to the magazine, he claimed he had spoken "nothing but Indian" for about 15 years. A year later, on November 12, 1930, he first used the name Grey Owl. And, by February 1931, he was telling his editors at *Country Life* that he had Native blood.

By that time, he was also using the Ojibwa version of his name, although his spelling of it was inconsistent: at a Montreal forestry conference in January 1931, he signed Wa-shee-quon-asier; in his book *Men of the Last Frontier*, the name is Washaquonasin; but when *Pilgrims of the Wild* was published, the name was rendered Wa-sha-quon-asin.

According to biographer Donald Smith, the correct spelling is *washaquonasie*, the Objibwa word for screech owl. Literally, it translates as white beak owl, but Archie claimed it meant "he who walks by night" — a reference to his own nocturnal wanderings.

Whatever he called himself, Archie Belaney had always lied when it served his purpose. Although his bizarre behaviour suggested he might have had some difficulty telling fact from fiction, in actuality he seems to have understood precisely what he was doing. In the early 1930s, when writer Lloyd Roberts questioned him about his outrageous persona, Archie's explanation was straightforward — people would remember Grey Owl in his beads and feathers more vividly than a conventionally dressed woodsman. And if they remembered Grey Owl, they were much more likely to remember the beavers he was trying to save.

Ultimately, two factors probably enabled Archie Belaney to get away with his masquerade. First of all, as Canadian historian Pierre Berton observed, he looked and acted like a stereotypical "Hollywood Indian." In full costume, Grey Owl evoked all the romance and tradition of the "noble savage," obscuring the poverty and prejudice that affected most Native peoples of the era.

The second factor was his message. Time and time again, Archie's behaviour should have betrayed his origins. If he was Apache, as he claimed, why did he use the Sioux greeting *How Kola* to begin his British lectures? When Dr. T. W. Allison of the University of Manitoba reviewed *The Men of the Last Frontier* in 1932, he suggested that Grey Owl, as a Native, could not have written the book and concluded he must have had a ghostwriter. In March 1936, John Tootoosis, a representative for several Saskatchewan reserves, stayed with Grey Owl while visiting Ottawa. When he saw a small drum in his room, Tootoosis suggested that they sing together, and went first. When Grey Owl's turn came, it was immediately obvious that he was singing nonsense. Yet John Tootoosis said nothing, either out of politeness or out of respect for the work Grey Owl was doing.

A more public example was the Great Plains Indian convention at Fort Carlton, Saskatchewan, in August 1936. During the event, Grey Owl danced with hundreds of Cree, Assiniboine, and Sioux. Anyone watching would have seen that he was awkward and out of place — but no one commented publicly on the fact.

Perhaps there was behind-the-scenes speculation, but it was not until the *North Bay Nugget* printed its posthumous story that controversy erupted. Many of Grey Owl's erstwhile admirers were horrified. Not only had he fooled them by his masquerade, his personal life was scandalous. He had married four different women, fathered a son by another woman, abandoned three of his wives, committed bigamy, and wreaked havoc with his drinking and hell raising. Rather than being "a modern Hiawatha," Grey Owl epitomized the very worst that people believed about Native people — and then some.

Despite the scandalous revelations, many newspapers were sympathetic. "It is an odd commentary," wrote the *Winnipeg Free Press*, "but true enough, that many people will not listen to simple truths except when uttered by exotic personalities."

A few months after his death, Archie's publisher, Lovat Dickson, published *The Green Leaf: A Memorial to Grey Owl*. In it he wrote, "I care not whether he was an Englishman, Irishman, Scotsman or Negro. He was a great man with a great mind, and with great objectives which he ever kept before him."

It would take years for the public to put his contributions in perspective, but by the 1960s and the resurgence of the environmental movement, Grey Owl was once more a hero.

Chapter 8
The Great Pretender: Ferdinand Demara

In 1951, Canadians were involved in the Korean War. Because there were many casualties, officials encouraged communications officers to focus on good news whenever possible. One of the best stories in this category involved HMCS *Cayuga*, which had left Esquimalt, British Columbia., in mid-June for a second tour of duty. Part of the crew's assignment was to help South Korean allies. Occasionally, this included providing medical services.

One stormy September day, the *Cayuga* encountered a number of wounded Koreans. Most of the men had only minor injuries, but three were seriously wounded. The ship's medical officer was called. Assisted by a couple of staff members, Dr. Joseph Cyr tended the less seriously wounded men on the open deck, in spite of the torrential tropical rain. Then he and his small team turned the captain's quarters into a temporary operating room.

The most seriously wounded of the trio had a bullet

Ferdinand Waldo Demara Jr., 1921-1982

lodged close to his heart. Dr. Cyr made an incision in the soldier's chest. As the ship pitched and tossed, he separated the patient's ribs, cleared away the blood, and removed the bullet. Then he turned to the other two men, one of whom had a serious groin injury, the other a collapsed lung. Through the night, the heavyset 29-year-old and his small team toiled, concentrating completely on the men in their care. When the young surgeon finally looked up, it was daylight. Noticing several crew members looking through the cabin portholes, he flashed them a smile and the V for victory sign that British prime minister Winston Churchill had made popular during World War II. To the Koreans, and to his shipmates, the young surgeon was a hero.

When the three patients were resting comfortably, Cyr retired to his cabin for some much needed sleep. He got up hours later, rested and refreshed, and immediately went to check on the men. To his surprise, they had already boarded their vessel and returned to the Korean island of Chinnampo. Apparently, they were well on the road to recovery.

A short time later, while HMCS *Cayuga* was in Japan, the story of Dr. Cyr's heroic shipboard operations caught the imagination of a naval public relations officer. He prepared a press release, which was sent to Canadian newspapers. When the *Cayuga* returned to Chinnampo, Cyr made a point of visiting his patients. They were all recovering well, but the man who had had a bullet in his chest was weak from malnutrition.

Appalled at the living conditions on the island, the industrious doctor decided something had to be done. He took a launch to the island whenever he was free from his regular duties and got to work. He provided medical care for the local civilians and soldiers, and also introduced a sanitation program. Once again, his efforts came to the attention of the navy's public relations department. Another glowing news release praising the doctor's compassion was issued.

Meanwhile, the story of the shipboard operations had reached readers in Canada. Most of those who read the newspaper report were suitably impressed. But one reader was extremely perplexed. She happened to be the mother of Dr. Joseph Cyr, and she had heard nothing about him joining the Canadian navy. So she called her son in Edmundston, New Brunswick, and was reassured that he was still a civilian and had never served aboard HMCS *Cayuga*. Mystified, the real Dr. Cyr notified the RCMP. Soon after, he received a photograph from Ottawa. According to naval records, the baby-faced man in the photo was Dr. Joseph Cyr, surgeon aboard the *Cayuga*. One look revealed the truth to the New Brunswick physician. The man staring out at him was Brother John, a novice Catholic monk who had been a close friend of the doctor until he had abruptly disappeared the previous March.

What the unsuspecting Dr. Cyr had not known at the time was that "Brother John" was just the latest identity of Ferdinand "Fred" Waldo Demara, Jr., a high school drop-out who reinvented himself any time the urge struck.

Fred was born in Lawrence, Massachusetts, on December 12, 1921. His mother was an American, but his father had Canadian ancestry. The personality traits that allowed Fred to camouflage his true colours and avoid unwanted attention began developing when he was still a boy. When it served his purpose, he could be friendly and outgoing — the proverbial life of the party. On the other hand, he could also be very reserved, avoiding close contact with other people.

Because he was frequently in trouble as a youngster, his exasperated parents sent him to a Catholic high school, hoping that the discipline and a dose of religion would curb his wild ways. The discipline didn't work, but the religion took hold. Even though he was extremely intelligent and had a photographic memory, he left school before graduating.

At the age of 16, young Fred decided to become a Trappist monk. He entered Our Lady of the Valley Monastery in Valley Falls, Rhode Island, and, as Frater Mary Jerome, tried his best to keep the order's rules, including the vow of silence. After two years, it was apparent he was not suited to this life, although some of his superiors felt he might indeed have a religious vocation.

He was given a letter of recommendation and told to present it to the Brothers of Charity in Boston. He was accepted there and posted to Montreal, Quebec. But again, within two years he was bored. He returned to his parents' home in August 1941 and looked for work locally. Although he lacked credentials, the 19-year-old managed to obtain employment as a teacher at Boyshaven, a home for boys in West Newbury, 24 kilometres from Lawrence.

Whether he got this job because of his charm or his inventiveness is not known; however, he seems to have thrown himself into it selflessly. With his parents' help, he also started a program to encourage community donations of money, clothes, and toys for the school. Although the scheme was successful, the school management had a complaint. It seemed to them that Fred's own pupils were benefiting more than the other boys. When the school's brother superior challenged Fred on the issue, the young teacher quit.

By this time, the United States was involved in World War II. In a fit of patriotic fervour Fred decided he would serve his country by joining the army. Not surprisingly, he quickly discovered he was not suited to army life. Taking decisive action, as always, the rash young private went AWOL. Under another assumed name, he then entered another Trappist monastery near Des Moines, Iowa. At Christmas, he went home to visit his parents, who informed him that the military police had been looking for him. Fred's father persuaded his errant son to turn himself in. This was good advice. Although there was nothing truly memorable about his appearance, Fred was six feet tall and weighed well over 200 pounds. He was not an easy man to miss.

Immediately after the holidays, he travelled to Boston to do just that. But along the way he changed his mind. Instead of getting off the train in Boston, he went on to New York and enlisted in the navy.

His naval training included a basic medical course. Fred enjoyed the work and he asked for additional courses. To his great disappointment, he was turned down because he lacked the necessary academic credentials. Infuriated, he decided to rectify matters by getting the best educational

qualifications he could. Typically, he chose a rather unortho-
dox method of doing this. While leafing through a catalogue
for Iowa State College, he read a profile of Dr. Robert Linton
French, an alumnus who had joined the navy.

Presenting himself as Dr. French, Fred wrote to the
college explaining that he was being considered for a special
assignment, and asked for help in getting transcripts and
other documents. The college obliged. Once he had the
papers, he made copies and replaced French's name with
his own. Then he applied for officer training. This time, he
was successful, but at the last minute Fred lost his nerve. He
decided to go AWOL again. But this time he did it in style.

To elude naval authorities, he staged his own suicide.
After dark one night, he went to the end of a pier in the navy
dockyard and placed a uniform and a hat on the ground,
along with a note which read, "I have made a fool of myself.
This is the only way out. Forgive me."

Very much alive, Fred headed west, brazenly using the
name Robert Linton French and claiming to have a PhD. in
psychology. Once more he entered a monastery, and once
more he was asked to leave. If he was deflated by this rejec-
tion, it didn't keep him down for long. He drifted to Chicago
and joined the Clerics of St. Viator, an order that prided itself
on its highly trained academics. Although his doctorate
was accepted at face value, "Dr. Linton" lacked training in
Catholic theology and was told to take graduate courses. So
he did. The tough curriculum included six subjects, among

them metaphysics, ethics, and cosmology. Fred got A's in all six.

His career as a Catholic intellectual looked promising. Fred now had everything he had worked so hard to get — the admiration and respect of his peers and a job in which he could help people. There was just one problem. Fred Demara got bored quickly. After a few months, he quit. At an age when most men would have felt lucky to be settling into such a prestigious career, he looked around for another challenge.

For a while, he worked in a hospital in Milwaukee. Then, having contacted Gannon College in Erie, Pennsylvania, he was invited to set up a psychology department there. As dean of the school of psychology, he taught a number of courses and also spoke to various men's and women's clubs. He was an entertaining and popular speaker, and became so highly regarded for his sound advice that he was persuaded to write a booklet, *How to Bring Up Your Child.*

Don't worry about spoiling children, the childless bachelor counselled his readers. Instead, shower them with unconditional love. Fred's parenting guidelines probably had their roots in his own childhood experiences rather than in any psychology book he had ever read.

Despite his popularity, Fred ran afoul of the college's administration. Being perhaps too bright and too restless, he often came up with unconventional ideas. But, instead of discussing them with his superiors or colleagues, he tended to run with the ideas on his own, regardless of organizational policy or budget considerations. Invariably, this caused friction. Rather than change his tactics, Fred chose to leave the dizzying heights of his ivory tower and move on.

After Gannon College, Fred found himself at St. Martin's Abbey and College, just outside Seattle, Washington, which was run by the Benedictine order. Before long, Fred had established St. Martin's Student Psychological Center, where he gave basic lectures on psychology and also provided counselling to college students.

He made a number of friends in the community, one of whom was the local sheriff. As a result of their relationship, "Dr. Robert Linton French" was made an honorary deputy, permitted to carry a gun and to drive a car equipped with a siren and searchlight. Although he had never masqueraded as a peace officer, the siren and searchlight would have appealed enormously to Fred's vivid imagination and penchant for role-playing. He also became a notary public and was about to be appointed a justice of the peace when his past — or at least part of it — finally caught up with him. The FBI arrested him for desertion from the navy.

The maximum penalty for desertion during wartime was death. Fred would have known this, but given his naval experience, his fascination with psychology, and his chutzpah, he also knew how to beat the system. Fred pleaded guilty with extenuating circumstances and was sentenced to six years in a California prison. In the meantime, the army was notified of his whereabouts. By the time they got in touch with prison officials, the charming, easy-going prisoner had acquired a reputation as a model inmate. The army decided to drop the desertion charges.

Fred Demara was released after just 18 months in jail. He walked away with nothing worse than a dishonourable discharge from the navy and the bonus of a one-way ticket to New York City — the place where he had signed up.

The ticket proved to be the passport to a new life — but not a life on the straight and narrow. Despite incarceration, Fred blithely continued to follow his own star. On the bus to New York, he struck up a conversation with a biology student from Asbury College, close to Lexington, Kentucky. The young man raved about one of his professors, Cecil Boyce Hamann, who, apparently, was a brilliant teacher but so shy that he seldom left the vicinity of the small college. Hamann's reclusiveness was tailor-made for Fred's purposes.

Under his own name, Fred got a job at the Massachusetts General Hospital Eye and Ear Infirmary in Boston. Then he used infirmary stationery and the forged signatures of several members of the staff to build up Hamann's already impressive credentials. Armed with these, he created a new identity as a zoologist who specialized in cancer research — despite the fact he had no special knowledge of either zoology or cancer — and knocked on the door of the Brothers of Christian Instruction in Alfred, Maine. Once more, he became a novice monk. Renamed Brother John, he was sent to a farm near Grand Falls, New Brunswick, for training.

There he met the man who would unwittingly provide Fred with his most daring persona, Dr. Joseph Cyr.

In early 1951, Brother John offered to help his new friend to qualify to practice in the United States. It's easy to guess why Fred suggested the idea and offered to help him with the paperwork. He had the connections, he explained. All he needed was Cyr's records, including his Canadian medical license. Without a second thought, Cyr provided his new friend with the documents. A short time later, the good brother abruptly left the area.

In March, "Dr. Joseph Cyr" walked into the naval recruiting station in Saint John, New Brunswick, and offered his services. The Canadian armed forces desperately needed qualified medical men, and it seemed Cyr was a perfect choice. He was sent to Ottawa and examined by a review board. "I passed the physical exam without taking off my clothes," Fred later recalled, "and they never even bothered to take my fingerprints." The next day he was welcomed into the navy as a surgeon-lieutenant. Normally it would have taken weeks to process his application, but the navy was desperate. Cyr was assigned to HMCS *Stadacona* in Halifax.

Fred had had some medical training during his time in the American navy, as well as some experience as a hospital orderly, but his knowledge was certainly not extensive enough to successfully masquerade as a surgeon. So, while filling his duties to the best of his abilities, he upgraded his medical knowledge by reading everything he could get his hands on.

Through his years as an impostor, Fred had learned to pick other people's brains and use their knowledge to keep up his masquerades. In the Canadian navy, one of the first things he did was to tell his commander he had been asked to write a little manual for use in New Brunswick lumber camps. As he explained, lumbermen worked in isolated, dangerous conditions far from any medical help. What they needed was a simple list of instructions that could cover most medical situations. Somehow, probably through a mixture of flattery and self-deprecation, Fred persuaded his boss to take over the task. The commander happily prepared the guidelines, totally unaware that they were for Fred's own use.

By May, Fred was aboard the aircraft carrier *Magnificent*. Although his medical knowledge had increased tremendously, he did not impress his commander, who felt the new surgeon lacked medical training, especially when it came to diagnosis. When Fred learned about his superior's opinion, he hit on a strategy that made it appear his skills had greatly improved. Every time he encountered a case he could not diagnose, he put the patient in quarantine in an isolated part of the ship, well out of sight of his busy commanding officer. There, with the help of liberal doses of penicillin and other antibiotics, the patient eventually recovered, even if Fred was not sure what had been ailing him in the first place.

On June 15, Dr. Joseph Cyr was assigned to HMCS *Cayuga*, then docked in Esquimalt, British Columbia. Three days later, the ship sailed for her second tour of duty in Korea.

A short time later, the doctor was faced with a serious medical emergency. Captain James Pomer had a badly infected tooth. Of course, Fred had no experience with dental surgery, but that didn't bother him. He gave himself a crash course, filled his commander with novocaine, and quickly removed the problem. Pomer told him it was the best extraction he had ever experienced.

As the tour of duty progressed, Fred gained confidence. By the time he had operated so successfully on the Koreans and become known for his work on Chinnampo, he was flying high. His captain trusted him and he was popular with crew mates, who admired his medical expertise and enjoyed his exuberant personality. He had reached the zenith of his career as an impostor.

Then the newspaper articles appeared.

When the real Dr. Cyr blew the whistle, naval authorities investigated. In October, a radio message was sent to HMCS *Cayuga*. "Captain's eyes only, have reason to believe your Medical Officer is impostor. Investigate and report." James Pomer was sceptical, but he followed orders and confronted his surgeon. Fred put on a great show of being hurt and angry. "You don't believe me!" he cried in anguish. Pomer was again taken in by the consummate trickster and promised to get to the bottom of the mess. Pomer was likely astounded when further information confirmed that his heroic young doctor was, in fact, Ferdinand Waldo Demara, Jr., an impostor with a lengthy criminal record.

When Fred realized his ruse had been discovered, he locked himself in his cabin. He drank rum and swallowed barbiturates in what may have been a suicide attempt. He was unconscious when he was put aboard a British ship for transfer to Japan.

From Japan, he was flown back to Canada under escort. On November 12, 1951, he appeared before a naval board of inquiry. Largely to save the navy embarrassment during wartime, no disciplinary action was taken, but on November 21, Dr. Joseph Cyr, a.k.a. Fred Demara, was given an honourable discharge and more than $1,000 in back pay.

Incredibly, Fred had beaten the odds again, but this public humiliation finally shook his enormous self-confidence. He spent the money on a drinking spree then went home to Lawrence, Massachusetts.

Throughout his life Fred had been torn between his religious vocation, his altruistic feelings, and the need to be respected, admired, and popular. His masquerade as Dr. Joseph Cyr had brought him more fame than he could have imagined. *Life* magazine, the most widely read photo journal of the era, bought the rights to his life story. But fame came with a high price.

He found other jobs, using his own name, but missed the excitement and danger that came with pretending to be someone else. Inevitably, he drifted back into his old ways. As Ben W. Jones he worked at a maximum-security prison in Huntsville, Texas, where he set up a recreational program for inmates and also provided psychological counselling. He was greatly admired by prisoners and staff — including the warden — for his enthusiasm, dedication, and kindness towards the men. Then one of the prisoners found the article about him in an old copy of *Life* — and Fred ran.

He drifted in and out of jobs for the rest of his life, never quite able to settle permanently or escape his past. In 1960, he got an acting gig and played a surgeon in the movie, *The Hypnotic Eye*. Surprisingly, given his various impersonations, he was a terrible actor. By 1961, his name was on the screen again — but not as an actor. Hollywood made a highly fictionalized movie of Fred's life; Tony Curtis played Fred. Appropriately, the film was called *The Great Impostor*. That was not the end of the U.S.'s fascination with Fred Demara. Two books were written about him. Amazingly, 30 years after the books were published, Fred's story inspired a television series called *The Pretender*.

Although the movie and books must have brought back memories of more exciting times, Fred chose to concentrate on the religious life. During the 1960s, he earned a certificate in Bible studies, and by the 1970s he was working as a Baptist minister and counsellor in Anaheim, California. Despite his challenging occupation, he was often lonely, and depressed. He was also plagued by health problems. On June 8, 1982, at the age of 60, Fred Demara died of heart failure.

Like many impostors, Fred Demara never seemed quite clear about right and wrong. He forged documents, stole money, wrote bad cheques, and otherwise flouted the law. Yet he was not motivated by monetary gain as much as the need to maintain whatever fictional personality he had concocted. And, underlying all those fictional personalities was a compassionate man with a deep spiritual hunger.

So, what motivated him to play so many different roles? A biographer once asked Fred that very question.

Fred responded quickly, and with a grin. "Rascality, pure rascality."

Afterword

As the stories in this book show, there are various reasons people choose to become impostors. Isabel Gunn masqueraded as a man so that she could accompany her lover to the Canadian northwest; James Barry hid a physical disability in order to progress in his chosen career; and, at first glance, Henri Le Caron seems to have changed his identity because he was a patriot. But a close examination of his autobiography suggests he also enjoyed the danger inherent in leading a double life.

Danger, whether in the form of physical harm or severe embarrassment, is something impostors learn to live with. Indeed, it seems to be one of the factors that influence certain individuals to lead double lives. They love the risk of potential discovery — not just for the thrill, but because each time they get away with another lie they prove to themselves that they are superior to the people they dupe.

That need to constantly remind themselves that they are superior reflects a deep-seated personality flaw most impostors share. Cassie Chadwick, Long Lance, Grey Owl, and Ferdinand Demara are all classic examples. Insecure and unhappy with the circumstances of their lives, they used their considerable wits and vivid imaginations to reinvent themselves as the characters they really wanted to be.

Certainly they were scoundrels, but most of them —
with the notable exception of William Townsend — also did
a lot of good in the course of their impersonations. We may
condemn them for their lies and lawbreaking, but we also
admire them for the audacity which allowed them to smash
social conventions and create personas that were larger
than life.

Acknowledgements

The author gratefully acknowledges the following sources, which provided quoted material used in this book:
Cole, J. A. *Prince of Spies, Henri Le Caron*; Crichton, Robert. *The Great Impostor*; Crosbie, John S. *The Incredible Mrs. Chadwick: The Most Notorious Woman of Her Age.*; Dictionary of Canadian Biography online; *History of Welland County, Ontario*; Holmes, Rachel. *Scanty Particulars: The Mysterious, Astonishing and Remarkable Life of Victorian Surgeon James Barry*; Le Caron, Henri. *Twenty-five Years in The Secret Service: The Recollections of A Spy;* Long, Sylvester. *Long Lance: The Autobiography of a Blackfoot Indian Chief*; McCarthy, Joseph. "The Royal Canadian Navy's Mystery Surgeon" in *Grand Deception*; Messenger, Thomas. *The Lives, Trial, Confession and Execution of John Blowes & Geo. King...; Narrative of the Life of the Daring Murderer, Highwayman & Burglar, William Townsend; Newark Advocate*; Newman, Peter C. *Company of Adventurers*; Smith, Donald B. *From the Land of Shadows: The Making of Grey Owl* and *Long Lance: The True Story of An Impostor*; Winnipeg Free Press.

For Further Reading

Cole, J. A. *Prince of Spies, Henri Le Caron*. London; Boston: Faber and Faber, 1984.

Crichton, Robert. *The Great Impostor*. New York, Random House, 1959.

Holmes, Rachel. *Scanty Particulars: The Mysterious, Astonishing and Remarkable Life of Victorian Surgeon James Barry*. London, England: Penguin Books, 2002.

Smith, Donald B. *From the Land of Shadows: The Making of Grey Owl*. Saskatoon: Western Producer Prairie Books, 1990.

——. *Long Lance: The True Story of An Impostor*. Toronto: Macmillan of Canada, 1982.

About the Author

Cheryl MacDonald has been writing about Canadian history for nearly 30 years. A long-time resident of Nanticoke, Ontario, she is a full-time writer and historian whose weekly history column appears in the *Simcoe Times-Reformer*. Her historical articles have appeared in *The Beaver*, *Maclean's*, the Hamilton *Spectator*, and *The Old Farmer's Almanac*. Cheryl has written 26 books on Canadian and Ontario history, including Amazing Stories titles *Niagara Daredevils*, *Deadly Women of Ontario*, and *Celebrated Pets*.

A member of the Professional Writers Association of Canada and the Canadian Authors Association, Cheryl is currently completing a master's degree in history at McMaster University, Hamilton. She can be contacted through her Web site: www.heronwoodent.ca.

Index

Index

Photo Credits